HISTORY, PHILOSOPHY AND SOCIOLOGY OF SCIENCE

SOCIOLOGY OF SCIENCE

Classics, Staples and Precursors

HISTORY, PHILOSOPHY AND SOCIOLOGY OF SCIENCE

SOCIOLOGY OF SCIENCE

Classics, Staples and Precursors

Selected By

YEHUDA ELKANA
ROBERT K. MERTON
ARNOLD THACKRAY
HARRIET ZUCKERMAN

MATTER & GRAVITY
IN NEWTON'S PHYSICAL
PHILOSOPHY

By

A. J. SNOW

ARNO PRESS
A New York Times Company

New York — 1975

Reprint Edition 1975 by Arno Press Inc.

Copyright © 1926, by Oxford University Press
Reprinted by permission of
  The Clarendon Press Oxford

Reprinted from a copy in
  The University of Illinois Library

HISTORY, PHILOSOPHY AND SOCIOLOGY OF SCIENCE:
Classics, Staples and Precursors
ISBN for complete set: 0-405-06575-2
See last pages of this volume for titles.

Manufactured in the United States of America

————◆————

Library of Congress Cataloging in Publication Data
Snow, Adolph Judah, 1894-
  Matter & gravity in Newton's physical philosophy.

  (History, philosophy, and sociology of science)
  Reprint of the 1926 ed. published by Oxford University
Press.
  Bibliography: p.
  1. Newton, Sir Issac, 1642-1727. 2. Matter.
3. Gravitation. I. Title. II. Series.
QC16.N7S56 1975   531.'5   74-26293
ISBN 0-405-06619-8

MATTER AND GRAVITY
IN NEWTON'S
PHYSICAL PHILOSOPHY

Oxford University Press

London   Edinburgh   Glasgow   Copenhagen
New York Toronto Melbourne Cape Town
Bombay   Calcutta   Madras   Shanghai
Humphrey Milford Publisher to the UNIVERSITY

MATTER & GRAVITY
IN NEWTON'S PHYSICAL
PHILOSOPHY

A STUDY IN THE
NATURAL PHILOSOPHY
OF NEWTON'S TIME

By

A. J. SNOW

Lecturer in Psychology
Northwestern University

OXFORD UNIVERSITY PRESS
LONDON: HUMPHREY MILFORD
1926

PREFACE

In this essay an attempt is made to study the most important and critical period of natural science. Although, therefore, dealing mainly with Newton, I have felt that some detail in regard to the points of view of other important writers of Newton's time would be useful. From time to time, accordingly, a detailed discussion of such writers is given, even though a strict adherence to the subject under consideration might have dispensed with it.

The author's special thanks are due to Professors W. T. Bush and M. R. Cohen, of Columbia University and of the College of the City of New York respectively; to the first for his kind interest in the author's work, without which it would never have been written, and to the second for suggesting and helping to clarify many details of the work; to Professor H. T. Costello, of Trinity College, Hartford, Connecticut, for helpful and

Preface

untiring advice and criticism. In particular, I have great pleasure in this expression of obligation to my colleague, Professor F. B. Kaye, who has read copy and proof and has made useful suggestions for improvement—suggestions that I have, in the main, adopted and embodied in the essay.

A. J. S.

Evanston, Illinois,
 July 1, 1925.

CONTENTS

8 *Contents*

IV

NEWTON'S METAPHYSICAL DOCTRINE OF GRAVITY

Contents 9

V

THE ROLE OF MATHEMATICS AND HYPO-THESIS IN NEWTON'S PHYSICS

INTRODUCTORY NOTE

In an age when physical science—in fact, all science—is once more critically examined, and when the adequacy of Newtonian mechanics is being questioned, it is fitting to discuss, even if it be fragmentarily, some of the fundamental concepts of Newton's physical philosophy. It is the doctrine of gravitation, and with that, naturally, the concepts of space, time, and mass, that are to-day especially attacked. Even though from the point of view of mathematical physics Newton's law of gravitation is clear, his attempt to give a metaphysical explanation of the causes of it is, to most students of the philosophy of science, very far from being clear.

In the study of this problem the student of Newton's natural philosophy is compelled to examine many complex problems which are related directly to it. For instance, the best approach to the problems involved is the study of Newton's conception of the nature and function of atoms, which, in turn, compels the student to investigate the influence of Newton's contemporaries and predecessors. Thus the Epicurean atomic theory was adopted through Gassendi by Boyle, who in turn somewhat influenced Newton, even though the latter was much more directly influenced by Galileo.[1]

Because Newton did not discuss directly the nature of atoms in his physics we will therefore study Newton's use of the concept of particles in his physical theory, and especially in his objections to Descartes's physics and astronomy. Because of Newton's definition of matter the following question forces itself upon us: If particles have the quality of inertia, and not motion, what is responsible for their motion? This question leads to a direct consideration of the main problem, which is: What is the cause of motion?

Newton's answers to the above question are first studied in the light of a kinetic theory;[2] and secondly with reference to the influence of Platonism[3] in order that we may gain a better understanding of its nature and mode of operation. These considerations lead us to an investigation of Newton's conception of natural laws, of absolute space, and of world-mechanism.[4]

Finally, the experimental and theoretical reasons for Newton's position becomes clear as a result

[1] Chapters I, § iii, and II, § ii.
[2] Chapter III.   [3] Chapter IV.   [4] Chapter V.

of the study of Newton's distinction between experimental philosophy and philosophy in general, which was connected with his conception of scientific method and of the nature and function of hypothesis.[1]

---

[1] Chapter V.

I

THE ATOMIC REVIVAL

It is an interesting historical fact that it was the mission of a Christian divine to rehabilitate Materialism. It was Pierre Gassendi who revived the Atomistic philosophy, and being a capable philologist he was no doubt familiar with the works of the ancients, and was able to choose therefrom that system of philosophy which was most adapted to his purpose. He was influenced also by Galileo's work. Being at heart an empiricist—or we may say, in a sense, a dogmatic 'sensationalist'—and a student of nature, he adopted for his purposes the Epicurean system.[1] Epicurean philosophy had been generally discarded by the philosophers, and not only discarded but scorned, because that philosophy was considered to be heathenism of the worst type. The opposition among philosophers to the atomic philosophy of the Greeks was dogmatic, emotional, traditional, and not scientific—in fact some

[1] Gassendi, P., *De Vita et Moribus Epicurei*, Leyden, 1647 (*Works*, Lyons, 1658).

scientists used the atomic hypothesis. However, the atomic philosophy, while not held by philosophers in general of the time, was far from dead; there were sufficient germs for a revival at the opportune time. First, the works of the ancient were available and read. Second, the way was prepared for modern atomic science by Bruno and Basso. Third, the opposition to the Aristotelian philosophy, which was beginning to lose its hold upon thinkers, such as Lips, Schoppe, Sennert, Magnenus, de Bérigard, and Maignanus, made it imperative to turn to other sources of inspiration, which led naturally to Epicureanism. Already we have Bacon regarding Democritus, and not Aristotle, as the ancient philosopher; [1] and of course Epicurean metaphysics was based on Democritus. Fourth, the atomic theory, as we have mentioned above, was used by the best of scientists—Galileo.

Such were the factors which produced an environment favourable to the great revival of atomism. The general historical background may be best studied in the theories of three leading exponents of atomism—Gassendi, Boyle, and Galileo.

---

[1] *Novum Organum*, Book I, Parts 51 and 63.

§ I

The John the Baptist of the revival, Gassendi,
like Lucretius, the Epicurean poet, admitted the
necessity of indivisible elements, even though his
reasons for that conclusion were different from
those of his predecessor. Lucretius thought that
there were two reasons for this doctrine. First,
because things are more easily destroyed than
reconstructed, he believed that the divisibility of
atoms must have limits ; for, if there were no
limit to the divisibility of atoms, the process of
dissolution in the course of endless time would
proceed so far that the restoration of things would
become impossible. Lucretius, it should be remembered, lacked our conception of the in-
finitesimal. He believed that infinite divisibility
meant ultimate disappearance. To him, therefore,
the fact that particles do not disappear had to
mean that they were not infinitely divisible.
Secondly, Lucretius held that infinite divisibility
would be incompatible with the laws governing
the production of things, because, if they were not
made up of minute indestructible elements, all
things might arise without any fixed law and order.

Gassendi was not interested primarily in atoms,
but rather in the significance of atomism. He
asserted that magnitude, figure, and weight are
the properties of atoms, and that lightness is not

a quality, but a relative weight. The first two—magnitude, figure—were recognized by Democritus, and the third—weight—was added by Epicurus. Weight, or resistance, on the other hand, is not so much a property, Epicurus thought, as *ipsammet corporis tribus reliquis subiectam naturam* ; that is, it is nothing but solidity.[1] ' But, as a matter of fact,' Gassendi says, ' the attribute of " form " or figure is not an intrinsic attribute of matter ; matter in itself is without figure or " form " ' ; but again, ' " form " never exists without matter ; it is matter which is fundamental and unchangeable, while " form " changes constantly.' Consequently, he concludes, matter in itself is both indestructible, and incapable of being produced by man, since God is the only one who can create it, and nothing can be born out of nothing.[2] So Gassendi argued that atoms are the ' reals ', in so far as we are concerned with the world of objects and the category of quantity. These ' reals ', or atoms, are for Gassendi homogeneous in substance but vary greatly in figure ; they are composed of parts, which are the *materia prima*, but yet there is no

[1] Lange, F. A., *Geschichte des Materialismus und Kritik seiner Bedeutung in der Gegenwart*, Leipzig, 1898, vol. i, p. 108.

[2] *Syntagma Philosophicum*, in *Works*, Lyons, 1658, vol. i, p. 266. Gassendi agreed on this point with Galileo.

void between the parts in the atom ; they are merely *mathematically* infinitely divisible,[1] but *in reality* indivisible. The figure of the atom, Gassendi thought, is due to the particular combination and number of its parts ; the formation and disintegration of objects is due to the union or separation of atoms, which in turn, as has been stated, are also made up of parts. All the compounds, objects, or bodies composed of atoms, Gassendi says, are in constant motion—a motion which does not cease when the bodies come to rest.[2] Gassendi never mentions that there is motion within the atom.[3]

Because of the fact that atoms aggregate to form bodies, and also because atoms are in constant motion, Gassendi argues that there must be a place into which the atoms move which is devoid of atoms. There must consequently be a void, and this vacuum is just as much a primary part of the universe as the atoms, although its function is different. The nature of the void, he

[1] Here we may notice the influence of Descartes. See below, Chapter I, sect. ii.

[2] Here Hobbes and Gassendi agree, as also does Leibniz, who asserts in his *Hypothesis Physica Nova* (1671) the continuity of motion by means of the idea of tendencies to motion (*conatus*) throughout the smallest movements and in the smallest parts. See below, Chapter I, sect. ii.

[3] *Syntagma Philosophicum, op. cit.*, vol. i, sect. i, Bk. III.

thought, is rather a condition than a cause, and only atoms are capable of constituting *res generabiles*.

What causes this motion Gassendi does not say definitely. If any one had asked him, ' Why do bodies fall to the earth ? ' Gassendi would have said, ' It is because of attraction by the earth.' What is that attraction ? His answer would have been indefinite, if not ambiguous. The one thing he was sure of was that the attraction could not be *actio in distantia*. He was sure also that it was not a primary quality of the body. There must be some influence, he reasoned, which reaches over to the object and pulls it to the earth. This influence would seem to originate from the earth, because the object in itself would have no desire to fall towards earth. The favourite analogy that Gassendi used in his endeavour to explain this attraction is the magnet. Just as the magnet draws iron to itself, so the earth draws things to itself,[1] he declared. But this ' influence ' or ' drawing towards ' should not be interpreted to mean that the magnet or the earth throws out hooks or hands with which to pull its respective objects ; rather, Gassendi explained, there is an influence of

[1] *Syntagma, op. cit.*, i. 337, 345. In this connexion it may be remembered that Gilbert (see above, Chapter IV, sect. i) used the same explanation, speaking of the earth as a great magnet.

the same nature as that manifested by a boy being attracted by a good piece of cake.

In considering the analogy of attraction between the earth and the magnet it may help to see in more detail what Gassendi understands by the magnet's power of attraction. In his main discussion of the phenomena of the magnet, under the head of ' Inanimate world ', [1] the magnet seems to have a mystical relationship with a higher form of existence. If a magnet comes within the range of iron it exercises the capability of drawing the iron towards itself by some invisible power. This attraction is physical ; consequently, he reasoned, it cannot be attraction at a distance, but rather mediated action, and this mediation is accomplished by a *substantialis corporeusve effluxus.* Furthermore, the magnet, for Gassendi, bears an analogy to sense and to plants. This analogy to sensible beings has four aspects : (1) As a boy is attracted by a piece of cake, so iron is attracted by a magnet. (2) In both cases a specific power or influence is emitted by the cake or the magnet. (3) In both cases this power enters into the ' soul ' of the object (boy or iron), and by causing a disturbance produces the movement. (4) This motion begins in both cases in

[1] *Manet vero solum locum discriminationeque ministrat, op. cit.,* vol. ii, sect. iii, Part 1.

what Gassendi refers to as ' soul '. As for the analogy that a magnet bears to a plant, it is the likeness of habit. As a tree can be grafted only in one way, so the magnet can be united to another magnet only as the fibres of the magnet run.

The language of Gassendi, at this point, seems animistic ; but after all, Gassendi, speaking about the soul of a magnet, modifies the word *anima* by a qualifying *quasi*, while the soul of, let us say, a boy, he calls *anima sentiens*. Being always anxious that the reader shall not mis-understand him, he is careful to point out that the magnet has only ' something analogous to a soul '.

Because of its bearing on our later discussion it may be well to say a word or two here about Gassendi's notion of light. Light in itself is a corporeal substance, according to his notion, ap-parently much like an aggregate of corpuscles, or rays formed of corpuscles. These corpuscles, as such, independent of individuals perceiving them, are merely *existentia* ; but when they are per-ceived—when they produce the sensation of light in us—they are merely *complexa*.[1] As to the origin of light, Gassendi confesses his ignorance.

Gassendi, unlike the ancient atomists, did not

[1] Cf. *ibid.*, i. 429.

think that out knowledge is complete when we have accomplished a qualitative analysis; he assumed, as most contemporaries did, that he could go back to the first course of things. He emphatically denied that the atoms are eternal and infinite. Gassendi was a dogmatic ' sensationalist ', but he always maintained the existence of a Being not perceived through the senses; he held, that is, that God, the Soul of the World, is the one cause which has no body; that God, who is over and above the material universe, is the Creator of atoms in space and time, space and time being *sui generis*; and that God put the atoms into motion. Gassendi never regarded atomism as an anti-religious doctrine—although to others atomism has so often seemed thus; nevertheless the secondary causes which follow are in all other respects self-subsistent and exclusively corporeal.

Robert Boyle continued the revived atomic philosophy, saying, in his essay on the ' Origin of Form and Qualities ', that he gained more from Gassendi's exposition of the Epicurean philosophy than from a long study of the numerous opponents of Aristotle, and he called his own way of thinking *philosophia corpuscularis*.[1]   Boyle, like Gassendi,

[1] The Oxford Dictionary mentions Boyle as the first one to use these terms.

was an empiricist and a lover of experimental truth, always ready to adhere to experimental results in preference to those derived from ' pure reason '.

Boyle agreed that there is one ' catholick or universal matter ' which is common to all bodies. This universal matter, he thought, is a substance which has three main characteristics ; namely extension, impenetrability, and divisibility. As to the first two characteristics of this substance he agreed with Gassendi, whereas the last one, which he attempts to reconcile with the other two, he borrowed from Cartesiaus.[1] Since this substance is homogeneous, Boyle then has to ask, How is diversity of bodies possible ? ; and this question led him to look further for a principle which is responsible for the heterogeneity of bodies. It cannot be due to the matter itself, he thought ; ' since we see not how there could be any change in matter, if all its (actual or designable) parts were perpetually at rest among themselves, it will follow, that to discriminate the catholick matter into a variety of natural bodies it must have motion in some or all its designable parts. . . . But, since local motion, or an endeavour

---

[1] 'A Discourse of Things above Reason', in *The Works of the Honorable Robert Boyle*, in six volumes, a new edition, London, 1772, vol. iv, pp. 408–9.

at it, is not included in the nature of matter, which is as much matter when it rests as when it moves ; and since we see that the same portion of matter may from motion be reduced to rest, and after it hath continued at rest, as long as other bodies do not put it out of that state, may by external agents be set a-moving again ; . . . ' I think ' that the origin of motion in matter is from God ; and not only so, but think it very unfit to be believed that matter barely put into motion, and then left to itself, should causally constitute this beautiful and orderly world : . . . '[1]   So matter and motion—' two grand and most catholick principles of bodies '—being granted, it naturally results that matter can actually be divided into parts, the dividing ' being the genuine effects of variously determined motion ' (as with Descartes).   Each of these fragments, ' or other distinct and entire masses of matter ', must have two attributes, their own individual magnitude—that is, size— and their ' singular ' figure or shape.   And furthermore, experience points, especially in chemical operations, to the division of matter into ' corpuscles or particles ' which, though material, are not objects of sense.   From this we may infer that the smallest fragments as well as the largest

[1] ' The Origin of Forms and Qualities, according to the Corpuscular Philosophy,' *op. cit.*, iii. 15.

aggregates of matter are likewise ' endowed ' each with its own individual figure and peculiar size. For, being finite, each and every body must have some finite and determinable size and figure; although the size or figure may change, yet at each particular instant it must always have some determinate magnitude and shape. Consequently, Boyle thought, we must attribute three essential properties to the corpuscle or particle; namely, magnitude or size, shape or figure, and either motion or rest.[1] Boyle does not assume continuation of motion when the body is at rest,[2] as did Gassendi (see above, p. 18). Where several of these corpuscles unite, their definite position in space and order of combination must be taken into consideration. As with Gassendi, so with Boyle, matter is indestructible. Furthermore, because its particles can move, there must be empty space or void into which they can move. If we should ask Boyle, ' How is it possible that the variety of bodies that we see about us is the product of two and only two simple catholick elements '—matter and motion; what is the origin of all these diverse qualities that bodies manifest ? ' he would answer that it is very simple for the ' corpuscularian ' to reply to the above query. He would

[1] Cf. *ibid.*, iii. 16, 17.
[2] Influenced by Descartes; see Chapter I, sect. ii.

reply somewhat as follows : first it may be shown
how other ' catholick affections ' are deducible
from ' local motion '; and secondly, how these
' affections ' variously combined give rise to the
variety of characteristics seen in bodies.

These characteristics were seen by Boyle about
as follows : (1) ' Local motion ' must belong to
some parts of primary matter, and thus it has
different ' determinations ' in the different corpuscles that compose that matter ; consequently,
it follows that by this ' local motion ' thus
circumstanced, matter is divided into individual
parts, each of them being finite. (2) These
must then necessarily be of some finite *size*, and
(3) must have some determined *shape*. According
to Boyle, not all parts of ' universal matter ' are
always in motion, some being motionless by their
mutual implication, or have ' transferred ' (as far
as we may use the human organism as an analogy)
their motion to other parts of bodies, and consequently they are (4) in a state of *rest*. These
four properties—local motion, size, shape, and rest
—are the most primary and simple ' affections ' of
matter.[1] Secondly, from the above four primary
' affections ', there are others which naturally
' flow ', although they are not universal, but are,
nevertheless, general principles of the qualities

[1] ' The History of Particular Qualities ', *op. cit.*, iii. 297.

of bodies. Not only bodies, but also their parts, even the minutest corpuscles or particles, (5) bear certain particular relations to each other, such as of *posture* or *position* (e. g. they are erect, declining, horizontal, &c.), and in respect to the individual that may perceive them, (6) they bear the 'quality' of order or *consecution*. Accordingly, we say they are ' to the right ' or ' one behind another ', &c. (7) Any number of these corpuscles being ' associated ' together in order to compose a body have individual and peculiar ways of being related to each other, and we may label this manner of existing together their *texture*. And, because bodies generally, when they are in such composition, cannot come together completely, but only touch each other in parts (corpuscles being spherical or of some shape), they leave intervals between them, we may therefore say (8) that all such bodies have *pores* in them, and, because most bodies have this structure, they are easily agitated and separated into their constituent parts by heat and other agents ; therefore (9) these bodies will permit the storing and the emanation of those ' subile spirits ' commonly called *effluvia* (which really are responsible for the movement and change of bodies). Nevertheless there are certain types of corpuscles that adhere to one another, constituting more durable and not casually disintegrating bodies, 'that may be called the primary concretions or elements of thing,' and (10) this quality of corpuscles we may call *mixture* or *composition*. The difference between the qualities of mixture and texture is one of degree of stability of adhesion of elements to form a compound. Each body, whether great or small, whether it be a corpuscle or a mass of corpuscles of the greatest magnitude, bears a relation not only to each other and every other particle within the mass, but also, being a part of the universe, bears a separate and distinct relation to the whole of the cosmos, which is governed alike far or near. (11) This we may call the *universal fabric of things*, as by the laws of motion established by the author of nature (God) in the world, (12) and matter itself being the *general affection*. Boyle thus has twelve principles which are responsible for the variety of bodies in the universe. He proceeds to show in a more or less concrete way— as did Lucretius and others of old—how the production comes about of what may be almost an infinite variety of bodies. Just as, having only twenty-six letters in our alphabet, we may compose a great variety of words and expressions, so, with the twelve principal qualities of corpuscles, we may, through thus various relationships and combinations, constitute the great variety of bodies.[1] Let us take one example and see how Boyle shows that what seems a simple principle is actually capable of causing multiplicity of variation. 'Local motion' seems a very simple principle, and yet we experience a multiple diversity of moving bodies, and some move slowly, some more swiftly, forming between the two extremes of motion an infinite number of degrees of swiftness. Some bodies may move in a straight line, others in an infinity of possible curved lines. The motion may change and vary in the same continuous course of movement, because of change of friction or of collision with some other bodies. A body may move upwards or downwards, decliningly or horizontally, east, west, south, or north, south-west, &c. The same body may have more than one motion at the same time, and in different combinations. Within a body the corpuscles may move, in reference to each other, in all imaginable ways and directions, some slower and some faster, according to the number of passages or pores within the aggregate or mass. Such are some of the varieties of 'local motion'. This diversity of motion affects and changes a body, and this not only as regards its relation to other bodies, but also internally, as when one corpuscle changes in reference to another, and,

[1] *Op. cit.*, vol. iii, p. 298.

by doing this, changes the body in a multitude of ways.

But again, we may inquire of the corpuscular philosopher: How is it that, if all the variety of bodies is due to the four principal and universal qualities or affections of corpuscles—extension, impenetrability, divisibility, and motion—two bodies may agree in one quality, and, naturally in the structure upon which that quality depends, it does not follow that they ought to agree in other qualities too; since those also are inseparably bound up with the structure in so far as they agree; so that it would be impossible to imagine that two such bodies would manifest many different qualities? Yet this is what, as a matter of fact, they do. For example, let us suppose reflection is a result of the emanation of an innumerable number of the corpuscles of which glass is made. Now if this or some other mechanical fact is responsible for the reflection of both glass and diamonds, how is it that diamonds reveal altogether different properties of reflection from glass? The corpuscular philosopher would have to confess this a difficult problem, but he might attempt to meet this difficulty by the following four considerations.

First: Invisible and heterogeneous corpuscles sometimes may lodge within the pores of visible and stable bodies, and these are responsible for the peculiar qualities manifested by some bodies. For example, if we soak one sponge in water, the pores will be filled with water and the sponge will have the quality of dampness, whereas another sponge, which has not been soaked in water, will have the quality of dryness. Consequently, the wetness of the first sponge is due to the presence of corpuscles within the pores of the sponge and not to the mechanical structure of the sponge.

Second : If the combination of corpuscles composing a certain body should change, let us say by minute movements, or by juxtaposition, without noticeably changing the texture of the body, it might nevertheless change sufficiently so that it lost some qualities and gained others. We may cite as an example a cold body, which, through some external pressure, would become warm, yet still retain the general appearance of that body.

Third : As we have pointed out, the production of qualities of a body should not be considered in reference only to itself, i. e. to the structure and relationships that exist between its component parts, but also in reference to the whole universe of which it is a part.

Fourth : There is no reason why we should not suppose that corpuscles composing bodies may give birth not only to essential qualities arising from their texture, but also, without destroying that texture, produce a variety of additional and diverse qualities. This example ' may let you see the same body, which the chemists themselves will tell you is simple and homogeneous, may, by virtue of its shape and other mechanical affections . . . have such differing respects to different sensories and to the pores, &c. of diverse other bodies, as to display several very differing qualities. The example [we] speak of is afforded [us] by the distillation of putrefied urine, for though such urine has already lost its first texture before it came to be distilled, yet when it has undergone two or three distillations to dephlegm it, the spirits of it swimming in a phlegmatick vehicle have a pungent saltness upon the tongue, and a very strong and, to most persons, an offensive smell in the nostrils ; and when they are freed from the water, they are wont to appear white to the eye ; and to ery tender parts, as to those that are excoriated, or to the conjunctiva, they feel exceedingly sharp, and seem to burn almost like a candlestick ; . . . the same saline particles invisibly flying up to the eyes prick them, and makes them water ; and invading the nose often causes sneezing. The same corpuscles taken into human bodies have the qualities that in other

medicines we call diaphoretick and diuretick ; the
same particles being put upon filings of brass, produce a fine blue, whereas upon the blue or purple
juices of many plants they presently produce a
green ; being put upon copper, whether crude
or calcina, they do readily dissolve it, as corrosive
menstrums are wont to do other metals, and yet
the same corpuscles being blended in due proportion with the acid salts of such menstrums, have
the virtue to destroy their corrosiveness ; and
if they be put into solutions made with such
menstrums, they have a power, excepting in a very
few cases, to precipitate the bodies therein dissolved. And again, if we ' compound this urinous
salt with the saline particles of common salt . . .
these two being mingled in due proportion, and
suffered leisurely to combine, will associate themselves into corpuscles, wherein the urinous salt
loses most of the qualities [we] have ascribed to it,
and with the acid spirit, composes . . . a body
little differing from sal ammoniac ; which great
change can be ascribed to nothing so probable, as
to that of the shape and motion (not here to add
the size) of the [corpuscles of the] urinous salt,
which changes the one and loses a great part of the
other by combining with the acid spirits '. And,
answerable to our supposition, after we have
eliminated the superfluous, ' there remained in

the bottom a salt, not only far more sluggish than the fugitive one of urine, but whose visible shape was quite differing from that of the volatile crystals of urine, this compounded salt being generally figured, whether like combs or like feathers. . . . These extra-essential changes that may be made in the shape, contexture, motion, &c., of bodies, that agree in their essential modifications, may not only qualify them to work themselves immediately, after a differing manner upon differing sensories, and upon other bodies also, whose pores, &c., are differently constituted, but may dispose them to receive other impressions than before, or receive wanted ones after another manner from the more catholick agents of nature.[1]'

Boyle develops an elaborate doctrine concerning the ways in which one of the qualities of corpuscles called the ' effluvia of bodies ', may produce complex results. There are at least six ways by which the ' effluvia of a body ' may operate upon another body or corpuscle, ' namely ; (1) By the great number of emitted corpuscles. (2) By their penetrating and pervading nature. (3) By their celerity and other modifications of their motion. (4) By the congruity and incongruity of their bulk and shape to the pores of the bodies they are to act upon. (5) By the motion of one part upon

[1] *Op. cit.*, vol. iii, pp. 303–5.

another, that they excite or occasion in the body they work upon, according to its structure. And (6) by the fitness and power they have to make themselves be assisted, in their working, by the more catholick agents of the universe. . . .' One body, then, may act upon another, not necessarily in one way only, but in more than one way at a time.[1]

Boyle, like Gassendi, ascribes the creation of matter and motion to God.[2] God is not only the creator, but also the first cause, not only the ruler of the universe, but also and more especially one who is constantly supervising his work, and occasionally intervening, because a universe which is not supervised and interfered with from time to time by its Maker is a universe of a godless type. Boyle compares the universe with the ingenious clock of the Strasburg Cathedral, the clock being almost a perfect mechanism, made to serve a definite purpose, and retouched and amended from time to time whenever it fails to serve its purpose perfectly. Boyle does not seem to think that an all-powerful and all-knowing God would necessarily make a universe which would not need any interference on his part in order to fulfil the divine purpose of its Maker. Such stability

[1] ' On the Great Efficacy of Effluvia,' *op. cit.*, iii. 678.
[2] Cf. *ibid.*, iii. 15.

or equilibrium, if we may call it such, as the universe has is due to its geometrical structure —the universe is the embodiment of perfect geometrical construction.

The atomic theory as adopted by Boyle and Gassendi had, as I hope to show, an indirect influence upon Newton. Even though Newton followed in the footsteps of Kepler and Galileo, nevertheless Newton's use of the atomic theory was modified by the influence of Boyle. To that which Galileo used, and Boyle explained and developed, Newton gave a profound mathematical basis. This mathematical basis formed the ground for a physical explanation.

§ II

The revival of atomism by Gassendi was contemporaneous with and responsible for another and opposed development of conceptions in the field of physics—the Cartesian conception of matter. Atomism as propounded by Gassendi and Descartes gave rise to a lively dispute which formed Newton's intellectual background. René Descartes divided *res* into two highest substances, one intellectual (thought-objects, i. e. things pertaining to mind), and second, corporeal (things pertaining to matter). The modes of thinking-substances are two, i.e. perception, or the operation of the understanding, and volition, or the operation of the will. Thus sense-perception, imagining, and conceiving things that are clearly intelligible, are for him just different methods of perceiving ; but ' desiring, holding in aversion, affirming, denying, doubting, all these are the different mode of willing '.[1] The modes of material substance, on the other hand, are listed as ' extension in length, breadth, depth ', or thickness, figure, motion, position, infinite divisibility, &c.[2] Both thinking and material substances, Descartes says, have a principal attribute which is their respective nature and essence : the attribute of thinking-substance is thought, and the attribute of material-substance is extension in three dimensions. Every other quality or characteristic of substance, therefore, is the direct result either of extension or of thought. It is not true, he argues, as against Gassendi, Boyle, Henry More, and others, that figure, hardness, and finite magnitude are essential attributes of matter ; though they all agree that the corporeal substance does not consist in its being heavy or having some colour.[3] As regards figure, how can a material substance which is infinitely divisible have a parti-

[1] *Principia Philosophiae* (Part II, prin. 32), in *Œuvres de Descartes*, publiées par Ch. Adam & P. Tannery, Paris, 1905, vol. viii, p. 17.   [2] *Op. cit.* (Part II, prin. 53), vol. viii, p. 25.
[3] *Op. cit.* (Part II, prin. 4), vol. viii, p. 42.

cular figure ? Descartes, never thinking in terms
of atoms, naturally could not conceive of substances as having figure ; and, even granting that
they had figure, he believed that the figure would
change from time to time—as indeed his opponent
admitted. Neither, he reasoned, can material
substance have finite magnitude nor its particles
be indivisible, because the essence of this substance is by nature infinite and infinitely divisible
extension. However small the ' modes ', or
manifestations (atoms), of extended substance
may be, they are still divisible, because where can
we stop with the divisibility of matter when
its material substance is synonymous with extension ? Conceptually, then, extension implies
divisibility. Now to Descartes, that which is
conceptually distinct must be real. The modes of
extended substance, therefore, being distinctly
divisible in thought, must of necessity be divisible
in nature.[1] To put it in other terms, for Descartes the primary and absolute qualities of matter
are extension, divisibility, and mobility : from
these primary qualities it follows that ultimate
atoms do not exist. Matter being synonymous
with extension, there is no vacuum. The material
world is infinite, for it is impossible to limit
extension, and the changes in nature must be

[1] *Op. cit.* (Part II, prin. 20), vol. viii, p. 51.

explained according to the highest natural laws, and these are the mechanical laws of impact. Because this concept of matter points to the simplicity of nature we are compelled to admit that the whole universe bears also the mark of simplicity, and, consequently, it is simplest to suppose that the whole universe is a perfect mechanism.

This argument and concept of extension aroused many criticisms from the opposing school. Gassendi objected that what Descartes clearly saw as mathematical extension, and which he took as the basic principle of his physics, was nothing but his mere thought, and that it had no existence outside of his mind, ' being merely an abstraction that he formed from a physical body ; that, consequently, the whole of Descartes's physics is but imaginary and fictitious, as is likewise all pure mathematics ; and that the physical nature of the real things that God has created requires a matter that is real, solid, and not imaginary. Consequently, he reasoned, to say that material substance is infinitely divisible because mathematical magnitude is, is simply to imagine a fictitious magnitude which logically admits divisibility, but to identify this logical magnitude with physical matter is pure folly. To the above criticism, Descartes answered as follows : ' Here

we have the objection of objections, and the sum
of the whole doctrine of these men of great
acumen who are here brought into evidence.
Everything that we are able to understand and
conceive is, according to their story, but imagina-
tion—the fictitious creation of our mind—and
can have no real subsistence : whence it follows
that nothing exists which we can comprehend,
conceive, or imagine, or admit as true, and that
we must close the door against reason, and content
ourselves with being monkeys or parrots, and no
longer be men, if we wish to place ourselves on
a level with these acute intelligences.' [1] Gassendi's
objections reflected the influence of Galileo—an
influence clearly shown in the whole of Gassendi's
principles of natural philosophy. Like Galileo,
Gassendi started from the axiom that nothing
can become nothing, or can arise out of nothing,
and that therefore, throughout all change, something must persist. That something is matter—
matter made up of a manifold of solid and indivisible elements. To admit infinite divisibility
of matter would mean to them the reduction of

[1] Descartes's letter to Clerslier, 12 January 1646, and the
fifth set of objections and replies between Gassendi and Descartes. Descartes continues : ' But I have something substantial
wherewith to console myself, inasmuch as my critics here
conjoin my physics with pure mathematics, which it is my deepest
wish my physics should resemble.'

matter to nothing, because any existence must have a finite magnitude. Consequently, although mathematical division can be continued *ad infinitum*, physical divisibility, said Gassendi, has a definite limit. At this point we may see the difference between the two men : Descartes was a rationalist ; mathematical or logical deductions, even though physically unverifiable, had for him existential value ;[1] whereas for Gassendi, who was fundamentally an empiricist, logical deductions were useful providing they were not physically contradictory. As we shall see later, that is also really the fundamental difference between Newton and Descartes.

Gassendi, therefore, differed from Descartes in asserting that we must attribute more than extension and mobility to matter ; we must also, he demanded, attribute to it a certain definite hardness which is not further divisible. Furthermore, Gassendi, under the influence of Galileo and contrary to the teachings of Descartes, thought that it is not motion but the impetus to motion that is constant, that the impetus does not cease to exist when motion passes into rest. Leibniz, it may be said in passing, thought the same. Gassendi also, in contradiction to Galileo,

---

[1] See my paper, ' Descartes's Method and the Revival of Interest in Mathematics ', *Monist*, October 1923.

thought with Telesio,[1] that atoms possess some sort of feeling.

Another figure in the controversy, Henry More, even though influenced by Descartes's conception of the world-machine, nevertheless took issue with him in this—that only matter has the attribute of extension. More's letter to Descartes pointed to his general agreement with the latter's philosophy, stating that there are only two philosophies that he greatly admires—Plato's and Descartes's. Nevertheless, he could not agree with him, first, in his identification of matter with extension, and second, in the view that the brutes are automata. A discussion of More's objections to Descartes will follow later. What we wish to point out here is More's objection to Descartes's doctrine of the divisibility of matter, which was discussed by them with reference to the question of the identification of matter with extension. Matter is a substance, said More, like Gassendi, which consists of parts ' discerptible ' from one another ; but its final particles are ' indiscerptible '. More put his objection in the form of a syllogism : ' That which can actually divide, and in so far as we can divide it, is divisible into parts " indiscerptible "

---

[1] Höffding, *A History of Modern Philosophy*, New York, 1915, i. 97.

. . . But matter is actually divisible in so far as division can be made. Therefore, matter consists of "indiscerptible" atoms, and actually it cannot be divided, but, on the other hand, matter may be infinitely divisible intellectually. It is the essence of anything that exists, whether it be material or immaterial, to have some finite extension or measure. Because, to deny extension to any spatial existent, is to make it pure negation or non-entity, considering that there is no middle point between existence being extended or non-extended. Consequently, there must be some finite extension, such as cannot be any smaller, belonging to "indiscerptible" particles of matter.'[1] These More calls *monades physical.* More also thought that to define matter by extension is to invest it with eternal and immutable qualities.[2] The extension of a spiritual substance, on the other hand, implies neither divisibility nor separability into elements. It implies the 'absolute powers of self-contraction and dilatation', along with the 'relative faculties of penetrating, moving and altering of the matter'.[3]

---

[1] 'The Immortality of the Soul, so far as it is demonstrable from the knowledge of nature, and the light of reason,' London, 1713, Preface, Art. 3 ; *Enchiridion Metaphysicum*, London, 1671, pp. 131 ff.

[2] *Enchiridion Metaphysicum*, p. 131.

[3] More, H., *Antidote*, Appendix III, 1.

Unlike More, Leibniz agreed with Descartes in regard to the divisibility of atoms, but not for Descartes's reasons. Descartes believed atoms to be infinitely divisible because of a logical necessity. But that did not mean to him, as it did to More, that, if matter be infinitely small in the series of divisibility, it will not have any dimension, because, no matter how far we divide extension, the parts will always have some extension, even if they be infinitesimally small. Leibniz could not believe in absolutely hard (indivisible) atoms, because that would contradict the principle of the conservation of force or the continuity of force. This doctrine (continuity of the impact of motion) was really developed by Galileo and was supported by Gassendi. Perfect elasticity of matter was absolutely required for it, if the Leibnizian law of conservation of force (or, as he called it, *Vis Viva*) was to be left intact, since when the coefficient of restitution is less than unity as it is actually in practice, *Vis Viva* is lost; that is, to put it in the nearest modern terms, loss of the constancy of kinetic forces. Leibniz pointed out that the apparent loss is absorbed by the small parts of bodies, that is, transformed from molar into molecular motion.[1] When Huygens,

---

[1] *New Essays concerning Human Understanding*, New York and London, 1896, pp. 669–70; *Leibnizens Mathematische*

however, in this respect anti-Cartesian, pointed out that this is quite impossible if interaction be through impact, Leibniz simply evaded the issue by denying that there are any last elements of bodies.[1]

Huygens could not agree with the Cartesian doctrine that matter is extension ; bodies, he said, must have an order which can preserve their form and be mutually resistant ; bodies, therefore, cannot be divided infinitely. But Leibniz thought there is a breach of the law of continuity [2] in assuming infinite hardness and absolute indivisibility to emerge suddenly when a certain point is reached in division. This discussion as to the divisibility of matter formed an important phase of the intellectual background of Newton's time ; and, while not necessarily affecting Newton through such comparatively late participants as Leibniz and Huygens, did actually, through Descartes, Gassendi, and More, shape the ideas he inherited from Kepler and Galileo.

Another disputed doctrine of the time was whether vacuum exists. Descartes's doctrine of extension as the essence of matter naturally did

Schriften, herausgegeben von C. J. Gerhardt, 1850–63, vol. i, pp. 230–1.

[1] *Leibnizens Mathematische Schriften*, vol. ii, p. 157.

[2] There are other reasons, but of less importance to our discussion.

not leave any room for an absolute vacuum, or space empty of matter. If space has magnitude, that is extension, then it must be material or contain matter, he reasoned, for extension is virtually matter. It is contrary to reason, in his view, to say that there is a ' vacuum, or space in which there is absolutely nothing '.[1] Our belief in a vacuum, says Descartes, is due to an error which we have acquired from the beginning of our lives. Noticing that there is a difference between a vessel and its contents, we believed it is possible for God to remove the contents of the vessel without replacing it with another body. Descartes attempts to avoid this naïve belief by pointing out that there is no necessary connexion between the vessel and its contents, but rather that there is an absolutely necessary connexion ' between the concave figure of the vessel and the extension ' which must fill its cavity ; consequently, we cannot conceive a cavity ' without the extension which it contains ', because vacuum, which is ' nothing cannot possess extension '. If there should be nothing in the vessel, Descartes reasoned, its sides would immediately come into contiguity with one another, because, according to the Cartesian conception of matter, it is a contradiction in terms for two

[1] *Principia Philosophiae*, Part II, prin. 16, vol. viii, p. 49.

bodies to be apart from one another. Any distance between two bodies, as is postulated when we speak of a vacuum, necessarily implies extension between the bodies. But extension is the essence of matter. Consequently there is never vacuum, but always matter.[1]

Thomas Hobbes reinforced the arguments of Descartes. Hobbes thought that real space, particularly space void of everything, is ' an imaginary space indeed '—a mere phantasm.[2] In order to show that there is no vacuum he proposed the following experiment : Suppose we take a vessel full of water, of which the bottom is perforated and the mouth securely corked. The contents of the vessel will remain stationary within, but if the cork be removed the water will flow freely from the perforated bottom of the vessel, but when we again close the mouth the flow of water will immediately cease. The cause of this phenomenon is, thought Hobbes, that the water by its natural endeavour cannot descend driving the air surrounding the outside of the vessel before it, because there is no place for the air to go into. The only way the water will flow freely from the vessel is by permitting the air surrounding the

---

[1] *Op. cit.*, Part II, prin. 18, vol. viii, p. 50. Leibniz agreed with Descartes on this point.

[2] Hobbes, *Elements of Philosophy*, Part II, ch. vii, Art. 2.

vessel to enter through the opened mouth of the vessel, where it may take the place of the water that flows out of it. And this, Hobbes thought, is a ' sign that all space is full ', because, if there were a vacuum, the water, being heavy, would naturally pass downwards, because nothing could hinder it from passing freely through the empty pores in the air.[1]

Leibniz felt that the existence of a vacuum is conceivable, but he believed that wherever there is room God would have placed matter, because the more existence the better it is.[2]   God, said Leibniz, would never miss the opportunity to create.[3]   Furthermore, if we admit that space is an attribute, then of what can empty space be an attribute ? [4]

Descartes's denial of the existence of a vacuum created a sustained sensation among the atomists

[1] *Op. cit.*, Part IV, ch. xxvi, Art. 2.

[2] *New Essays concerning Human Understanding*, by Gottfried Wilhelm Leibniz, together with an appendix consisting of some of his shorter pieces, translated by Alfred Gideon Langley, New York and London, 1896, p. 157 ; *Die Philosophischen Schriften von G. W. Leibniz*, herausgegeben von C. J. Gerhardt, Berlin, 1875–90, p. 140.

[3] *The Philosophical Works of Leibniz*, with notes by George Martin Duncan, New Haven, 1890, pp. 240, 253 ; *Die Philosophischen Schriften von G. W. Leibniz*, pp. 356, 378.

[4] *Die Philosophischen Schriften von G. W. Leibniz*, vii, p. 372 ; *Philosophical Works of Leibniz*, p. 248. As a matter of fact Leibniz thought of space usually as a relation.

of England, of which one of the latter champions was Clarke. Samuel Clarke, for instance, argued at great length against Descartes. He maintained that it is evident from the operation of gravity that there is a vacuum, which really occupies, so to speak, a greater part of nature than matter does. Furthermore, he said, the reality of a vacuum may be demonstrated from the motion of comets ; we observe that the comets are in continual motion through the heavenly spaces ; consequently these spaces must be void of any sensible resistance, and it naturally follows that there is not matter in the spaces.[1] 'The immense space of the world is so far from being full of matter (which imaginary plenum is the sole foundation of the fiction of vortexes), that, on the contrary, space, which is filled with matter, bears no proportion at all to that immense space which is void of all matter.' [2]

We may mention here some other arguments

[1] Rohault's *System of Natural Philosophy*, illustrated with Dr. Samuel Clarke's Notes. Taken mostly from Sir Isaac Newton's Philosophy. Done into English by John Clarke ; London, Knapton, 1723, vol. i, ch. viii, Note 1. See also *A Collection of Papers which passed between the late learned Mr. Leibniz and Dr. Clarke, in the years 1715 and 1716, relating to the Principles of Natural Philosophy and Religion*, London, Knapton, 1717.

[2] Clarke, *op. cit.*, vol. ii, Part II, ch. xxv, Note 1. Apparently here Clarke uses the arguments of Newton, found in his *Principia*.

put forward by the believers in the existence of a vacuum, such as that repeated from Lucretius, that there must be vacuum in nature, because if there were none, movements of bodies would be impossible, since there would be no place for bodies to move into. Another argument is as follows : If two flat bodies be pulled apart the air will immediately rush in between them. But no matter how rapidly the air fills the distance between the two bodies, there will always have to be an empty space which the air is just filling up. Hobbes answers these and other arguments rather ingeniously, but we shall not take the time to state his replies.[1]

In place of the empty space of the opposing school of atomists, Descartes developed a theory of ether, or extremely fine ' splinters, which came into existence when the corpuscles were originally rounded. Space as a plenum is full of this all-pervading ' fluid ', which is in constant agitation, or whirling motion.

This doctrine of ether was also a source of controversy ; it brought forward voluminous arguments against it. Boyle objected to Descartes's explanation of electrical attraction by the intervention of ether particles, ' flashed almost like

---

[1] Hobbes, *Elements of Philosophy*, Part IV, ch. xxvi, Arts. 3 and 4.

small pieces of ribband,' [1] which are supposed to be the result of this ' subtile matter harboured in the pores or crevices of glass '.[1] Boyle is willing to grant the assumption as plausible, but he cannot admit its truth. For, if a solid body—for instance, glass—be rubbed for a few minutes against another of its kind, we shall find that it will not only emit ' effluvia, but such ones as to be odorous, and something to be rankly stinking '. This definitely shows that the attraction of bodies by the glass is not due to the intervention of ether particles, but rather to the emanation of an immaterial ' effluvium '. [1]

Again, the atomists asked of Descartes, ' If there is no vacuum, and all space is full of matter, how is motion possible ? ' Descartes answered his opponents by saying that all motion in the universe is impact motion. No motion can be produced without shock and contact ; the ethereal body which surrounds all bodies pushes them forward, just as objects heading towards a whirlpool are pushed towards the centre of it.[2] Descartes has two versions of his definition of matter : for the vulgar he defines it as ' *action by which any body passes from one place to another ;* '

[1] ' Of the Mechanical Origin of Electricity,' *op. cit.*, vol. iv, pp. 346-7.
[2] *Principia Philosophiae*, part III, prin. 46 ff., vol. viii, pp. 100 ff.

for the learned, Descartes defines motion as ' *the transference of one part of matter or one body from the vicinity of those bodies that are in immediate contact with it, and which we regard as in repose, into the vicinity of others* '[1]—the last definition of course, being the one prepared by Descartes. According to these definitions, a body may be said to change and not change its place ; that is, a man within a moving train is said to change his place in reference to the country he passes, but not in reference to the train which he occupies.[2]

All variety of matter, or all the diversity of its forms, depends upon motion. As we have said above, for Descartes all matter was homogeneous, its attributes being extension, infinite divisibility, and motion. All the varieties of properties and characteristics we notice in bodies, he thought, are due to the fact that matter may be divided and moved according to its parts ; all diversity of form depends upon motion.[3] The sum of motion is, said Descartes, always constant.[4] From this constant Descartes deducted three secondary laws : (1) that every body, if left to itself, continues in the state in which it is ; (2) that a body which

[1] *Op. cit.*, Part II, prin. 25, vol. viii, p. 53.
[2] *Op. cit.*, Part II, prin. 24, vol. viii, p. 53.
[3] *Op. cit.*, Part II, prin. 23, vol. viii, p. 52.
[4] *Op. cit.*, Part III, prin. 36, vol. viii, p. 95.

is moved maintains the direction in which it was set in motion, and moves in a straight line so far as it is not affected by extraneous causes ; and (3) that if a body which has been set in motion strike another body, a transfer of motion takes place.[1]

To this explanation of Descartes, as to his other aspects of his theories, objections were raised. Thus Hobbes believed that motion ceases to exist when the body comes to rest.[2] Gassendi and Boyle also took issue with Descartes's theory as to the cause of variety of bodies.[3]

Here again Hobbes re-enforces Descartes's doctrine of ether against the opposing doctrines of the atomists. There are three kinds of bodies, says Hobbes in one place—'*fluid*, *consistent*, and *mixed of both*. *Fluid* are those whose parts may be very weak and endeavour to be separated from one another ; and *consistent*, those for the separation of whose parts greater force is to be applied.' Therefore there are degrees of consistency, which we may call more or less hard or soft ; while a fluid body may be divisible into equally fluid bodies. The immense space of the universe is an aggregate of all kinds of bodies ; some are ' consistent and visible ', as, for example, the

---

[1] *Op. cit.*, Part V, prin. 37, 39, 40, vol. viii, pp. 61–7.

[2] *De Corpore*, 15, 2 ; 22, 1.

[3] See above, Chapter I, sect. i.

earth and the stars ; or invisible, as the ' small
atoms which are disseminated through the whole
space between the earth and the stars ; and
lastly, that most fluid ether which so fills all the
rest of the universe, that it leaves in it no empty
space at all '.[1] In another place Hobbes speaks, in
addition, of a fourth class of bodies, which are
intermingled in the air, being in a fluid state, but
' without that they are so small ', that we cannot
perceive them with our senses. In addition, these
bodies, like all other bodies, possess a simple
motion and several degrees of hardness.[2] But the
ethereal bodies, which apparently form a fifth class,
he continues, have no motion—' as if it were
the first matter '—but what they receive from
bodies which float in them and are not in themselves fluid.[3] Thus Hobbes agrees with Descartes
as to the existence of ether, disagreeing only in
assuming the ether particles to be in constant
whirling motion.

The final point of disagreement between the
rival schools was·that over mechanism. Descartes
explained the motion of bodies, whether of the
smallest particles of matter or of the largest
masses, whether organic or inorganic, by the

---

[1] *Op. cit.*, Part IV, ch. xxvi, Art. 4.

[2] *Op. cit.*, Part IV, ch. xxvi, Art. 4.

[3] *Op. cit.*, Part IV, ch. xxvii, Art. 1.

mechanical laws of impact motion defined above. Although he believed that God is the creator and the first cause of the universe, nevertheless he held that all bodies are subject to purely mechanical laws, that the whole world is a great and perfect machine created anew every moment.

Boyle and Clarke fought Descartes, saying that his philosophy was nothing but the grossest type of atheism.[1] Boyle and Clarke believed that the universe could never be adequately explained in terms of mechanism.[2]

We shall now summarize the controversy, both as to the position taken by Cartesians and the objections raised to them. For Descartes matter was an extended substance infinitely divisible, without finite magnitude or figure. To this concept of extended matter Gassendi objected, saying that infinite divisibility is only a mental abstraction, matter is atomic—here the influence of Galileo on Gassendi is clearly felt. More being influenced by Descartes in other directions, argued against him, saying that material substance is not the only one that has the attribute of extension Extension may also be an attribute of spiritual substance. However, Leibniz, like Descartes,

---

[1] Whereas More thought it the only philosophy which saves Deism.

[2] We shall discuss this objection more fully later.

argued for the infinite divisibility of matter, but for other reasons—because hard atoms contradicted the doctrine of the conservation or continuity of force. Descartes's doctrine of matter did not leave any room for the existence of a vacuum. In this he found support in Hobbes and later in Leibniz. In the anti-Cartesian quarters in England, Descartes again found stormy opposition. In the place of empty space the Cartesians proposed the theory of a phenum. Finally, Descartes found opposition in such men as Boyle, and later in Clarke, to his doctrine of mechanism. Descartes explained all motion— great or small—to be due to the mechanical laws of impact. Such was the intellectual background of Newton's conception of matter.

§ III

Gassendi's revival of atomism as filtered through Boyle formed a sort of intellectual atmosphere for Newton's atomic theories. But it was chiefly an atmosphere : the roots of Newton's conceptions were furnished by Kepler and Galileo ; the Gassendist revival with its attendant disputes was on the whole chiefly a factor affecting the development of these roots into the growth of Newton's speculation.

Kepler established that a body cannot of itself

pass from rest to motion. Galileo discovered the
next step—in the problem of bodies in motion—
that a body can neither change its motion of
itself nor pass from motion into rest [1]—conceptions which were to give rise to the Newtonian
law of inertia, which was not expressed as a general
law by Galileo. Movement is a primary quality
for Galileo. It is due to the movement of the
parts of the bodies that the physical appearances
are to be explained.[2] When a body exhibits
qualities which it has never possessed before it is
very likely due to a change in the dispositions of
the parts of the body, in which nothing perishes
and nothing is born. Nothing can come out of
nothing, nor can a body be annihilated, thought
Galileo, as Lucretius did before him. Qualitative
changes were intelligible to Galileo if traced to
quantitative factors. This of course means that
there is motion in space. The qualities of matter
must therefore appertain to motion, and these
must be corporeal.[3]

With the radically new conception of the world
due to the Copernican astronomy and the contributions of Bruno and Basso, the problem of

[1] Mach, *Science of Mechanics*, Chicago, 1907, p. 143. See
also Wohlwill, *Zeitschrift für Völkerpsychologie*, 1884, vol. xiv,
pp. 365–410, and xv, pp. 70–135, 337–87.

[2] Gassendi, Boyle, and Newton felt the same to be the case.

[3] *Il Saggiatore*, 1632, vol. ii, p. 340.

the nature and validity of knowledge came to the foreground—a problem which never existed for the Scholastics. If the picture derived immediately from our senses does not give us the true picture of the world, how can we get the true picture, and what is the relation of the one to the other ? In this problem of dualism there is for Galileo a decided difference between ' opinion ' and ' knowledge '. But that difference—between ' opinion ' and ' knowledge '—disappears more and more, the closer we come to having a mathematical knowledge of the universe, he believed. In this knowledge the human mind is governed, according to Galileo, by the necessity with which God thinks the truths which underlie the contents of nature. But that which we know only through mathematical deductions God knows intuitively, Galileo believed—thinking that human knowledge, limited and imperfect, approached God's in so far as disciplined by ' intensity, strictness, and necessity '.

In order to understand Galileo it is necessary to understand Galileo's distinction between knowledge and opinion, or, in other words, between objective and subjective, absolute and relative, mathematical and sensible, between what Newton was to call ' true ' and ' apparent '. The man in the street, the pure scientist, or even the mathematical scientist, can put in terms of a general statement, a law, or a mathematical equation, the impressions that things make upon his senses. The confusion of relative space with absolute space, time, and movement is due to the assumption that the sensed object is the metaphysical, mathematical, real object. We are in danger of thinking of common motions as metaphysical motions. Galileo, like Newton, believed that a distinction must be made between the mathematical point of view and the point of view of common sense.[1] The man in the street and the mathematician study the same object even if they do not describe it in the same way. One point of view can be derived from the other. The distinction is not made to separate the rational notions from the common, but to prevent the likelihood of ascribing to the latter a capacity that they do not possess. That was the first time in the ' modern ' history of philosophy that a real distinction between the metaphysical and sensible was made.[2] Between *natura naturata* and *natura naturans* distinctions were drawn.[3]

We are able now to understand the distinction

[1] Spinoza and Malebranche also felt that there is a difference between time and eternity. But while for Newton, as for Galileo, absolute time is mathematical and measurable, for Spinoza and Malebranche absolute time was not at all measurable.

[2] Between the real and the sensible there was common distinction in Greek philosophy—Eleatics, Plato, &c.—even Epicurus.

[3] Since the time of Galileo and Newton, and the Greek

that Galileo made between the primary and
secondary qualities of matter—a distinction which
had a great influence upon all subsequent science
and most philosophy through its adoption by
Newton and later by Locke. As we have stated
above, Galileo believed that all qualities apper-
taining to motion and to attributes of matter must
be quantitative and corporeal. These primary
qualities are figure, magnitude, and motion or rest.
Newton accepted all of these qualities but the
last one. These qualities are real, or, as Galileo
called them, *primi e reali accidenti* ; that is, they
cannot be by any exertion of our powers separated
from bodies. The secondary qualities are not
attributes of matter ; they are psychological. It
is the senses which make us regard smell, colour,
warmth, as absolute or real qualities. These are
only names we give to things because they excite
certain psychological reactions in us.[1]

atomists before them, absolute space, time, and movement,
which were derived *a priori* by the Cartesians, have tended to be
considered the only metaphysical realities. It is because we need
one scientific generalization for many facts that the common
notions or qualities can never be regarded as scientific. Furthermore, mathematical demonstrations give certainty because the
necessity in the universe is of a geometrical nature. *Two new
Sciences by Galileo Galilei*. Translated by Henry Crew and
Alfonso De Salvio. Macmillan & Co., New York, 1914, pp. 90–1
and 113. Descartes also distinguished between primary and
secondary qualities.

[1] *Opere di Galilei*, Florence, 1842–56, vol. iv, pp. 332–8.

It is because the primary qualities are not psychological that they can be reduced to movements and expressed in mathematical terms. Consequently the primary qualities—the attributes of matter—are figure, magnitude, motion, and rest. New bodies arise because of quantitative changes among these attributes, and consequently change can be mathematically expressed and predicted. All change is reduced to quantitative motion in space. It follows therefore, according to Galileo, that motion itself does not remain constant, but the impetus does so even when motion passes into rest. It also follows that matter is atomic, the atoms being indivisible and infinitely small. Although a line of any magnitude can be divided indefinitely, matter cannot.[1] In all of the above Galileo had a direct influence upon Newton, with two exceptions. First, Newton would not admit that motion is an attribute of matter. Secondly, Newton, like Descartes, did not believe that it is the impetus of motion that remains constant throughout all change.

[1] Galilei, G., *Two New Sciences*, p. 41.

§ IV

The discussion so far has been primarily historical, dealing with the development of atomism in the century preceding Newton's writing. In the next chapter we shall attempt to state Newton's positive position.

It may be of advantage to review some of the facts which are a part of the foregoing discussion. The atomic theory was invoked by Gassendi, and even by Galileo, not because of his special interest in atomism, but rather because it lent itself to proving or disproving certain other doctrines that he was primarily interested in.[1] The same may be said of Newton's use of the atomic theory. Epicurean atomism could be used to advantage in opposing Aristotle; and also, by its use, all change in nature could be reduced to motion and expressed in mathematical generalizations. The discussion of the divisibility of matter seems to have been, for the most part, even if not consciously so, a debate whether mathematical or logical deduction has existential value; at least that was uppermost in the mind of Gassendi. It was only Leibniz and Huygens who saw the real physical significance of the question whether matter is infinitely divisible. For them hard

----

[1] The same was the case with Epicurus.

atoms would not permit the elasticity which was necessary in order to have force conserved. On the other hand, the Leibnizian objection to the existence of a vacuum was naïve and theological. That God is the creator of all things and the first cause was accepted by all dogmatically. However, the idea that the universe is actually like a machine once for all put in motion by God was fully accepted only by Leibniz. Descartes and Boyle admitted that the world is like a machine ; nevertheless they believed God close by, in order to have it created anew every moment (Descartes), or retouched and amended from time to time whenever it failed to serve its purpose perfectly (Boyle). More, however, saw theism safe with the world machine, whereas Gassendi, Newton, and Clarke were afraid that this would lead to atheism, and argued consequently that the world is not actually or metaphysically a machine. They all agreed, however, that the universe is the embodiment of a perfect geometrical construction. While Galileo and Descartes thought of motion as a property of matter, Gassendi, Boyle, and More thought of motion as coming from the outside of matter. Attraction or motion is like magnetic force, or like the force that moves the ' boy toward an apple ' ; it is *substantialis corporeusve effluxus* (Gassendi), and ' emanation of an immaterial effluvium ' (Boyle, More). Newton seems to have had similar metaphysical ideas about motion. Descartes, however, thought that motion is purely physical, transmitted by ether through impact.

With the above intellectual background in mind we are now ready to discuss more fully Newtonian Atomism, which constitutes the subject-matter of the next chapter.

II

NEWTONIAN ATOMISM

§ I

In the preceding chapter we have indicated
that Newton's nation of atoms was a direct and
natural development of Galileo's position, but
influenced somewhat by Boyle, with whom he
was intimately associated, Boyle being influenced
in turn by Gassendi's revival of atomism and by
the controversy between the schools of Gassendi
and Descartes. Such was the positive ancestry
of Newton's atomism. But it is important to
know not only what ideas Newton borrowed, but
what conceptions he reacted against and opposed,
since, by acting as an irritant to his speculation,
these rejected conceptions served as a stimulant to
further development of the conceptions he had
taken over. The great negative influence of this
kind on Newton's atomism was Descartes's physics
and astronomy.

Before the appearance of Newton's *Principia*,
and even for some time after, Descartes's physics
occupied the most prominent position among
the learned men of Europe. The new Copernican

system demanded a new celestial mechanics, which was apparently supplied by Descartes. This system was rapidly accepted, and in the English universities it seemed to hold an undisputed sway with the exception of Cambridge, where it had been recently introduced by Isaac Barrow.[1] Newton was a pupil of Barrow. Newton studied and expressed his appreciation of the new Cartesian geometry,[2] which helped make Newton's immortal work possible.[3]

Why did Newton find it necessary to refute Descartes's system and construct one of his own ? The reasons were many and diverse. First : Newton made a clear distinction between experimental philosophy and philosophy in general, and was always conscious of it in adopting any scientific supposition which by its very nature could not be *experimentally* proven. Descartes never made such distinctions. Second : Newton thought that his scientific observations contradicted some fundamental principles of Cartesian physics. Third : according to Newton, Cartesian

[1] Mabilleau, Léop., *Histoire de la Philosophie atomistique*, Paris, 1895, p. 153. See also Rohault, J., *Tractatus Physicus*, London, 1682.

[2] Brewster, David, *Memoirs of the Life, Writings, and Discoveries of Sir Isaac Newton*, Edinburgh, 1855, vol. i, p. 22.

[3] Newton, however, never regarded Descartes's geometry as highly as he did Euclid's.

mechanistic philosophy not only failed to give a direct proof of God's existence, but really left no place for God.[1] Fourth : the corpuscular philosophy of Galileo, Newton thought, was, on the one hand, better adapted for a theistic doctrine of the cosmos, and, on the other hand, its employment could, better than anything else, serve the purpose of describing the whole universe in terms of mathematical relations. We shall now consider the above-mentioned reasons.

Newton's first objection it will be more convenient to treat later. In order to be able fully to understand Newton's second objection, it will be necessary to state Descartes's astronomical theory.

Descartes dealt only with two of the four scholastic categories [2]—quantity (extension), and motion. Descartes gave up his early definition of motion—that is, ' action by which a body passes from one state to another '—and adopted a new one, as he expressed it, 'the transformation of one body to the body nearest it '—impact motion.[3] From this definition of motion, he deduced his three

[1] Of course Descartes's proof of the existence of God did not lie in the field of physics.

[2] The scholastic categories are quantity, place, time, and motion.

[3] *Œuvres de Descartes*, edited by Charles Adam and Paul Tannery, vol. viii, p. 53 ; vol. i, pp. 26–9.

laws of motion.[1] Seven rules follow these three
laws.[2]

Descartes, as others in his day, regarded the sun
as at the centre of the solar system. The earth
is not isolated, but, on the contrary, it is the
centre of a fluid matter, which is in a state of
constant whirling motion—is a whirlpool or
vortex. This fluid matter surrounds the earth
completely, and it is this vortex which moves
around the sun and carries the earth with it ; the
earth in reference to this surrounding fluid being
perfectly stationary. Analogously, if a piece of
straw moves with a stream of water, the straw is
purely ' passive ' and stationary in reference to the
water : the water, moving along, carries the
piece of straw with it. A body is in motion when
it will successively occupy the positions of other
bodies nearest to itself, these in turn displacing
others, until some sort of circuit is completed, each
member of the cycle simultaneously moving into
the place of the next. All this may be said of the
motion of the earth. Then it follows from this
description of motion that the earth is at rest if

---

[1] See above, Chapter I, sect. ii. These rules were never
understood, in all probability, not even by Descartes, who never
regarded them as important to the understanding of his physics.

[2] Neither of these sets of laws is found in his work upon the
world.

we regard the immediately adjacent bodies, for it is at the centre of a fluid vortex moving round the earth, by which vortex the moon, or rather the moon's vortex (as explained below), is carried around the earth as centre. But though the earth does not move with reference to the vicinity of bodies composing this earth-vortex—and thus it can be truly said that the earth is ' at rest ' [1]—the entire vortex with the earth within it, does move, carried in a larger vortex round the sun, so that the earth changes its position with reference to the sun.

With this vortex hypothesis Descartes attempts to explain the tendency of bodies to fall toward the earth if they are suspended in the air, providing that they are not hindered in doing so by other bodies. Just as any freely moving light body—for example, a straw—caught in a whirl-pool or eddy of water, will finally be whirled into its centre, so any object freely suspended in the air of the ' earth-vortex ', or small vortex immediately surrounding the earth and carried with the earth in the large vortex round the sun, will tend towards the centre of the ' earth-vortex '. The earth being the centre of that vortex, quite naturally all the bodies coarser or greater than the

---

[1] *Œuvres de Descartes*, edited by Charles Adam and Paul Tannery, vol. viii, pp. 97, 98, 124, 125. For a diagram of Descartes's astronomy see vol. viii.

matter of which the vortex is composed will fall to its centre.

From the eclipses of the moon and of the sun, from the size of the moon, and from the intensity of its reflected light, we may infer that the moon is not far from the earth. Therefore it is natural to suppose that the moon's vortex is contained in the vortex of which the earth forms the centre. And because the fluid matter of the vortex moves from west to east it carries the moon along with it. But the circle described by the moon is larger than that of the earth, the earth making one complete revolution in reference to its axis in one day, while the moon takes twenty-eight.

When fixed stars become opaque they cease to be permanent centres of any vortex, and they pass from one vortex to another which is immediately next to it, and so on still to another, continuing this movement ; these stars we call comets.[1]

The celestial system contains, all told, fourteen vortices. The vortex containing the sun is the largest of all ; there are six vortices of the planets, one of the moon, four of the satellites of Jupiter, and two of Saturn. The planets move more rapidly the nearer they approach the sun.[2]

[1] *Œuvres de Descartes*, edited by Charles Adam and Paul Tannery, vol. viii, pp. 168–91 ; vol. ix, pp. 172–90.

[2] *Ibid.*, vol. ix, Part I, p. 197, and Part II, p. 196.

As a matter of fact this hypothesis is one of many possible ones, thought Descartes, in so far as the Creator of matter and motion display a gradation of relations. This hypothesis is not the first one nor the last one—and what the first one was like we do not know. Therefore, in so far as this supposition is not the primitive one, it is not the primary and true one, but rather a naturalistic hypothesis of physics.

Descartes supposed that fine corporeal substance formed extremely small bulbs, which are violently moving, and, among these, circulates fluid matter, which is still finer and moving still faster, and here and there are centres about which the vortices are formed and are constantly moving.[1] All celestial spaces are filled with this thin fluid matter, which forms into vortices with large masses of matter at their centres.[2] This assumption of space-filling, thin fluid was forced upon Descartes, he believes, because of absolute necessity in astronomy. The evidence in astronomy makes such an assumption indispensable : action extending over enormous distances presupposes that space is ' compact '.

It was in relation to this astronomical theory

---

[1] *Ibid.*, vol. ix, Part II, pp. 324–5.
[2] *Ibid.*, p. 325 ; vol. vii, p. 89.

that Newton raised his second main objection to Descartes—that his astronomy was contradicted by experimentally derived facts. He said that he endeavoured to investigate the properties of the Cartesian vortices, in order to see whether the celestial phenomena could be explained thereby, and concluded that they could not be so explained, for the following reasons :

(A) Newton's objections involved the following astronomical data : the periodic time of the satellites revolving about the planet Jupiter are in the sesquiplicate ratio of their distances from the Jupiter's centre ; and the same rules hold true, with the greatest accuracy, between the revolving planets about the centre of the sun. Therefore, if these satellites are carried in their respective vortices about Jupiter, and within Jupiter's vortex about the sun, then the vortices must also follow the same rule of revolution. But, as a matter of fact, the ' periodic times of the parts of the vortex ' are in the ' duplicate ratio of the distances from the centre of motion ; and this ratio cannot be diminished and reduced to the sesquiplicate ', as the vortex theory would necessarily demand, unless either the matter of the vortex would proportionally become more and more fluid the further it is from the centre, or the ' resistance arising from the want of lubricity in

the parts of the fluid, should, as the velocity with
which the parts of the fluid are separated goes on
increasing, be augmented with it in a greater
ratio than that in which the velocity increases '.
But the unreasonableness of these two require-
ments is apparent. The ' more gross and less '
parts of the fluid will tend towards the cir-
cumference of the vortex, unless they be heavy ;
then, naturally, they would tend towards the
centre of it. And even when Newton supposes
that the resistance is proportional to the velocity,
though—as a matter of probability—the resistance
is in a less ratio than that of the velocity, the
periodic times of the vortex from the centre will
still be in a greater ratio than the duplicate of the
distances. And yet some Cartesians—to make the
case still more hopeless—think that the parts of the
vortices move more swiftly at the centre, then
again slower as we travel outwards, and again
swifter as we approach the ' outskirts ' of the
vortex. And if it be so, then surely neither the
sesquiplicate (the ratio of the cube of a number
to its square), nor any other uniform ratio, can
hold true of its motion.[1]

(B) If any small part of a vortex, whose particles

---

[1] Newton, Sir Isaac, *Mathematical Principles of Natural
Philosophy*, vol. ii, pp. 195–6 (Book II, sect. ix, pp. 52 ff.).
English translation by A. Motte, 1st ed., London, 1729.

are in particular relation among themselves, be supposed converted from a fluid to a solid condition, then this small part will move according to the same rule as before, since no change takes place in its density, ' *vis infita,* or figure.' And again, if this solid part in a vortex, being of the same density as the rest of the vortex, be resolved into a fluid, this same part will again move according to the same law as it did in its solid state, but its parts, being now in a fluid state, will revolve and move among themselves. The motion of the ' small part ' will be the same as before, neglecting the motion of its individual parts, which do not affect the motion of the whole. This solid, now being like the other fluid of the vortex, will move as the rest of the vortex in so far as that is at equal distances from the centre. Consequently any solid, if it be of the same density as the rest of the vortex, will move with the same motion as the rest of the vortex does, ' being relatively at rest in the matter that surrounds it '. But if the solid part be more dense, established laws of mechanics enable us to deduce that it will endeavour to leave the centre of the vortex, revolving out of the centre in a spiral, and consequently would no longer be retained in the same orbit, and therefore overcoming that force of the vortex by which—the Cartesians thought—

the whole vortex is kept in a perfect equilibrium. It is also now apparent that a more rare part of the vortex, if it be solid or rare, must be of the same density as the fluid, in order to remain in the same orbit ; but if it be so, it would have to ' revolve according to the same law with those parts of the fluid that are at the same or equal distances from the center of the vortex '. All this is contrary to the Cartesian hypothesis, which assumes that solid bodies occupy the centres of vortices, and so we may conclude that the planets are *not* carried about the sun in *corporeal* vortices.

(C) The Copernican system, which Descartes claims he accepted, assumes that the planets describe ellipses in their revolutions about the sun, the sun being a common focus, and ' by radii drawn to the sun, describe areas proportional to the times '. But the motion of the parts of the vortex will not follow the above rule. Let three circles, of variant diameter, represent three orbits of revolving planets about the sun. The orbit having the greatest diameter is concentric with the sun, while the other two have independent centres, successively to the right of the sun, of variant distances from the sun so that they will form an aphelion to the right of the sun and a perihelion to the left of the sun. If these three orbits are symbolized by the first three letters of the alphabet, each successive letter corresponding with each successive orbit in the order of greatness of the diameter, the circle with the smallest diameter will have its corresponding letter 'A', &c. According to the rules of astronomy, the planet revolving in the orbit 'B' will move more swiftly in its perihelion and more slowly in its aphelion, whereas, according to the rules of mechanics, 'the matter of the vortex' ought to move faster in the narrow space, aphelion, and slower in the wider space, perihelion. Therefore it is apparent that the rules of mechanics and astronomy contradict the Cartesian system of vortices. 'So, at the beginning of the sign of Virgo, where the aphelion of Mars is at present, the distance between the orbits of Mars and Venus is to the distance between the orbits at the beginning of the sign of Pisces, as about three to two; and therefore the matter of the vortex between those orbits ought to be swifter at the beginning of Pisces than at the beginning of Virgo, in the ratio of three to one. For the narrower the space is through which the same quantity of matter passes in the same time of one revolution, the greater will be the velocity with which it passes through it. Therefore the earth, being relatively at rest in this celestial matter, should be carried round by it, and revolve together with it about the sun ; the velocity of the earth at the beginning of Pisces would be to its velocity at the beginning of Virgo in a sesquilateral ratio. Therefore the sun's apparent diurnal motion at the beginning of Virgo, ought to be above seventy minutes; and, at the beginning of Pisces, less than forty-eight minutes. Whereas, on the contrary, that apparent motion of the sun is really greater at the beginning of Pisces than at the beginning of Virgo, as experience testifies—therefore, the earth is swifter at the beginning of Virgo than at the beginning of Pisces.' Consequently, the vortex system of Descartes is 'utterly irreconcilable with astronomical phenomena '.[1]

(D) Because we notice the regular movements of our planets, Newton finds in this another objection to all-pervading-material-fluidity-of-space. 'For thence it is manifest that the heavens are void of all sensible resistance and, by consequence, of all sensible matter.' [2] Or, as he wrote on another occasion : ' I cannot admit that a subtle matter fills the heavens, for the celestial motions are too regular to arise from vortices, and vortices would only disturb motion.

[1] Newton, Sir Isaac, *Mathematical Principles of Natural Philosophy*, vol. ii, pp. 196 ff. (Book II, sect. ix, prop. 53), English translation by A. Motte, 1st ed., London, 1729.

[2] Newton, Sir Isaac, *Optics*, London, 1906, twenty-eighth query.

But if any one should explain gravity and all its laws by the action of some subtle mediums, and should show that the motion of the planets and comets was not disturbed by this matter, I should by no means oppose it.'[1]

(E) It is evident from the motion of comets that they could not be carried by a vortex, because they cut the orbits of the planets in all manners of angles and times.[2]

(F) Newton objected to making matter continuous, arguing that, if it were so, free movement would be impossible. But, as a matter of fact, bodies do move and change positions in all sorts of ways ; therefore it follows that space is not full of matter, but there are also vacuums into which matter can move.

(G) If all space were equally full, ' then the specific gravity of the fluid which fills the region of the air, on account of the extreme density of the matter,' would be about the specific gravity of quicksilver, or gold, and therefore could descend

[1] Leibniz requested Newton's opinion concerning Huygen's material in the appendix, ' Discours de la Cause de la Pesanteur,' to his *Traité de la Lumière* of 1690. On 26 October 1693 Newton favoured Leibniz by giving the above-cited reply.

[2] Clarke states the above as an objection of Newton, but we have to take this with caution. Clarke's notes to Rohault's system, *Tractatus Physicus*, London, 1682, Part II, ch. xxv, note to Art. 22.

in air.   Bodies which are lighter do not descend in
fluids.

(H) ' And if the quantity of matter in a given
space can [as Descartes says], by any rarefaction,
be diminished, what should hinder a diminution
to infinity ? ' [1]

It is owing to the development, by Newton, of
the notion of universal gravitation, that Descartes's
hypothesis of vortices falls, and with it the whole
astronomical structure.

Newton's third objection to Descartes's mechanistic philosophy was theological.   In this he
agreed with most of the Cambridge men, who
looked upon Descartes's mechanistic explanation
of the movement of the planets and of gravitation
as pure and simple atheism.   Though More felt
theism to be safe only within the Cartesian
mechanism, even he lodged strong objection to
certain phases of Descartes's mechanistic explanations,[2] while Boyle [3] and Clarke [4] in defending and

[1] Newton, *Mathematical Principles of Natural Philosophy*,
vol. ii, p. 224 (Book III, prop. 6, cor. 3).   English translation
by A. Motte, 1st ed., London, 1729.

[2] More, Henry, *Enchiridion Metaphysicum sive De Rebus Incorporeis*.   London, 1671, ch. 11 ; *The Immortality of the Soul*,
&c., London, 1713, Preface, 12.

[3] Correspondence between Boyle and More in Boyle's collected works, *The Works of the Honourable Robert Boyle*.   A new
edition, London, 1772.

[4] *A Collection of Papers which passed between the late learned*

explaining Newton, protested strongly against the Cartesian ' world machine '.

Newton's objections as to this point were three-fold. In the first place, Newton objected to the possibilities which Descartes's system allowed of banishing God. It is true that Descartes, in order to have the atoms stable and imperishable, granted to God the function of continual creation. But Newton felt that Descartes's world-machine was so mechanically self-sufficient that the relation to it of God as continual creator was merely a superstructure. To Newton, God was so essential that His constant providential interference was necessary for all phenomena, from the movements of the planets in their orbits to the history of a single atom. In the second place, Newton objected to Descartes's method of inferring meta-physical propositions from scientific propositions. Newton felt it essential to keep the spheres of metaphysics and of science distinct.

Newton did not want to rest the existence of God upon scientific deductions, feeling that that is not the way to get at metaphysical knowledge. Metaphysical [1] (philosophy in general) proposi-

Mr. Leibniz and Dr. Clarke, in the years 1715 and 1716, relating to the principles of Natural Philosophy and Religion. Knapton, London, 1717. See especially pp. 151, 351.

[1] Newton never used the term metaphysics; our use of the term here with reference to Newton is explained fully in Chapter V.

tions are never deduced from scientific propositions, he reasoned, for metaphysical deductions
follow the scientific ones only when *all* the
scientific knowledge is known and ordered ; they
are the last deductions in a series of deductions.
Scientific knowledge as we have it at present in its
incomplete form is never metaphysical knowledge,
from Newton's viewpoint.   While science describes the secondary causes or the relations in
mathematical form, it never is able to give us the
real and final causes, which are metaphysical.
Newton preferred dogmatically to infer the
existence of God from certain physical facts, not
as a scientific proposition, but rather in the form
of a question, a suggestion which cannot be
scientifically proved—which can, at best, be
asserted in the form of a corollary to physics.[1]
In other words, Descartes's mechanistic explanation, although useful for isolated facts, is yet not
a true *metaphysical* explanation for the cosmos
as a whole, for a complete and sweeping knowledge
of the universe would show it not as a mechanism
but as a providential arrangement.

[1] Newton accepted God as the first cause, dogmatically
holding that God's being intelligent makes physical science possible because He guarantees the stability of the cosmos : it is
the stability and the regularity of the universe that calls for the
existence of a God who is its first and final cause. This contention
receives justification and fuller treatment in Chapter V.

Newton never separated astronomy from the other sciences or mechanics from geometry : they were all one universal science, an experimental or natural philosophy, a unity of sciences. The real distinction that he made was between the sciences, or ' natural philosophy ', and ' philosophy in general ', or natural theology. He applied the same method to all facts in so far as these facts could be controlled by one unity. Indeed, a science which is composed of disjunctive parts was for him not a real science, for it lacked unity and simplicity. This distinction—which allowed escape from theology—and experimental method were, of course, responsible for the great scientific progress. From then on, as we know, science began to develop at a previously unknown rate.

The world for Newton was geometrical primarily but theological. Newton thought that his *Principia* would point to the necessary existence of God.[1]

Newton's fourth and final reason for refusing to accept Descartes's astronomy was that the corpuscular or atomistic philosophy of Galileo, he thought, was better adapted to a theistic

[1] General scholium at the end of Newton's *Principia* ; his letter to Bentley ; Cotes's preface to the second edition of the *Principia*. ' Voltaire, toujours aussi profond, s'écriait que les athées n'avaient qu'à écouter le grand homme, qui démontrait Dieu en observant les astres '. See Mabilleau, Léop., *Histoire de la Philosophie atomistique*, Paris, 1895, p. 446.

doctrine of the cosmos, and because its employment would better serve the purpose of describing
the whole universe in mathematical functions.
Newton's reasoning was as follows :

(A) By adopting Galileo's and Gassendi's
atomic hypothesis, Newton could very nicely
employ it in favour of theism. If atoms are
inert, then movement must come from other
sources. Also, if matter is atomic and there are
empty spaces, how can bits of matter attract each
other across void ? Surely not in terms of direct
contact and impact motion, nor is it *intelligible to
suppose they really attract each other at a distance*.
It might be by some non-material means which
moves and attracts matter. According to Descartes, movement is transmitted by impact ; the
only movement that takes place is that among
solid bodies, and that is to say translations and
rotations. The movement is conserved as long
as it is transmitted in the form of shocks. But
Newton thought that the movement due to the
propagation of light cannot be explained in terms
of shocks of solids, as will appear in Chapter III.

(B) Descartes, in order to be able to think of
matter in an objective sense, applied the doctrine
of simplicity of nature, reasoning about as follows :
If we try to think how things are constituted apart
from the way in which they affect us, we come

upon three characteristics, and these are extension, divisibility, and mobility. These are the simplest and clearest ideas that we can have of matter, and if we think only of these, and these are purely geometrical qualities, we will be able to understand, by the use of logical deduction, all that happens in the material world. And if it follows from the ultimate qualities of matter that they are geometrical—that is, extension, divisibility, and mobility—then atoms in a strict sense do not exist, matter can be infinitely divided. Also if matter is primarily identified with extension, which really is space, then all space being matter if full, or, to put it in other words, vacuum cannot exist in nature. The material world must be infinite, for it is impossible to limit extension.[1]

Newton objected to Descartes's notion of matter, contending that only by identifying matter with purely geometrical characteristics is one led to believe that real atoms do not exist, and that matter can de divided indefinitely. Matter physically, Newton thought, has a limit to its division. Furthermore, as has been stated above, he believed that space is not full of matter, that there must be a vacuum into which bodies move

---

[1] More objected to matter being identified with extension. In fact he thought that immaterial substance has also extension as one of its attributes.

when they change their position, especially when
certain facts of nature enumerated above point
to the existence of a vacuum. However, Descartes
was close to atomism ; for hard atoms, small
round corpuscles may be substituted, which
remain, as a matter of fact, unchanged, and are
further divisible only potentially. In place of a
vacuum Descartes has extremely fine splinters,
which have been formed when the corpuscles were
originally rounded.

(C) The hypothesis of individual finite atoms
lends itself very nicely to a mathematical treatment of them. Galileo and Descartes defined
matter in objective terms, while Newton gave to
atoms a mathematical meaning, conceiving the
simple atoms as points, and the relations of atoms
to one another as geometrical relations. Newton
could very easily employ mathematics in order to
describe the material universe ; the material universe is thus supposed to be made up of a large
number of aggregates of atoms, the individual
atoms being so small that their size would be
negligible, and might serve very well as equivalent
to the mathematical concept of a point. Starting
in this way to conceive gravity in universal terms
as an explanation of the movements of planets as
well as of the fall of stones, the domain of mechanical physics is extended, and the world receives the

formal enunciation of the principles of celestial mechanics, which have found their theoretical and practical utility to this very day. They are mathematical definitions of physics, models of nature, which can be modified as the necessity for it develops.

§ II

Finding Descartes's theory of the plenum with its vortices unsatisfactory, Newton turned, as we have said, to Galileo and the revived doctrine of Epicureanism. Newton tentatively defined particles in the following words : ' By the points of which lines, surfaces and solids are said to be composed, are to be understood equal particles, whose magnitude is perfectly inconsiderable ' ; [1] and again, he said, ' finite particles are not moments, but the very quantities generated by the moments ; we are to conceive them as the first nascent principle of finite magnitudes '.[2] It is very difficult to set down a single and definite formulation regarding the nature of the New-tonian particles or corpuscles, because Newton never thought it important to treat this concept by itself. We find it used only here and there in his writings. Newton was interested in atomism only

[1] *Principia, op. cit.*, vol. i, p. 268 (Book I, sect. 12, pr. 73, Schol.)

[2] *Ibid.*, vol. ii, p. 17 (Book II, sect. W, Lemma II).

indirectly. He was concerned with it merely in so far as it could be made a tool useful to his concepts of physics.

The influence of Galileo can be detected in the method that Newton employed to determine the primary qualities of matter. By experience, we learn, said Newton, that an abundance of bodies are hard,[1] impenetrable, and possess extension; and, because the hardness, impenetrability, and extension of the whole body arises from the hardness, impenetrability, and extension of its parts, therefore we may infer the hardness, impenetrability, and extension of all primary or undivided particles of which the bodies are composed; and not only of bodies we actually feel, but of all material bodies. We also learn, he continued, from experience, that all bodies are movable, ' and endowed with certain powers (which we call the *vires inertiae*) of persevering in their motion or in their rest ', and also we infer, as before, that this mobility and inertia of any body is due to its particles, which themselves have these qualities of mobility and inertia. The knowledge that the primary qualities of atoms include extension, hardness, impenetrability, density,[2] mobility, and inertia

[1] *Optics*, 3rd ed., p. 364.
[2] *Principia, op. cit.*, vol. ii, p. 224 (Book III, prop. 6, cor. 3 and 4).

is, Newton thought, the foundation of all philosophy.[1] Like Galileo and Gassendi, Newton thought it experimentally true that we may divide bodies into their parts ; but he held that, although we may divide particles infinitely into lesser and lesser parts in thought, this is impossible physically.[2]

Newton discussed somewhat more fully the question of empty pores, which he considered a fundamental characteristic of matter. Bodies are more ' rare and porous than is commonly believed', because they possess ' empty pores ', said Newton. ' Water is nineteen times lighter, and by consequence nineteen times rarer than Gold. . . .' Therefore, Newton pointed out, gold is able to transmit through its pores ' magnetick effluvia and easily to admit quicksilver into its pores ', and water will pass through it. If we should fill a sphere made of gold with water,

[1] We must remember that, in Newton's time, philosophy includes also physics.

[2] *Principia*, vol. ii, pp. 293–4 (Book III, Rule 3). Pillon, F. (' L'Évolution Historique de L'Atomisme ', *L'Année Philosophique*, 1891, vol. ii, pp. 67–112), in praising Newton, said that it is a mark of a genius to refute the Cartesian notion of infinite divisibility of particles, because, by ascribing to particles a definite magnitude not further divisible, he preserved the unity and permanence of that concept. As has been pointed out above, however, long before Newton's time Gassendi argued against Descartes's doctrine of indivisibility of matter. See above, Chapter I, sect. ii.

Newton says, and then apply great pressure to the water, the water would pass through the gold, and ' stand all over its outside in multitudes of small drops, like dew, without bursting or cracking the body of the gold '. Consequently, bodies rarer than gold will possess more ' empty pores ' than gold.[1] Newton also thought that transmission of light is only possible because transparent bodies are very rare, and have a very large number of pores.[2] He thought it would be possible to see these particles or corpuscles with the improvement of microscopes.[3] These particles, he believed, are of varying sizes and irregular figures, some a thousand times smaller than the largest primary particles in existence, and the difference of colour is due to the size of these colour-producing corpuscles.[4] For that reason, he explained, we are able to conjecture the bigness of the component parts of natural bodies by their colours.[5]

So, to sum up Newton's view thus far, we may say any mass is an aggregate of particles, and the qualities of any mass are dependent on a function of the qualities and characteristics of its particles and their particular combination. But Newton

[1] *Optics*, London, 1704 ; Book II, p. 69 (Book III, Part III, Prop. VIII).

[2] *Optics*, 1704, Book II, p. 80. [3] *Ibid.*, p. 64.

[4] *Ibid.*, pp. 63–5.

[5] *Ibid.*, p. 58.

never said that mass is proportional to the quantitative number of its particles. Newton defined mass as ' the quantity of matter of a body, as measured by the product of its density and bulk (volume) '. This definition of mass, Mach [1] remarked, is an unfortunate one, for, ' as we can only define density as the mass of unit of volume, the circle is manifest.' However, if we consider the following syllogism, as suggested to me by Professor Henry Crew, we may notice that Newton did not reason as Mach charges : Take as fundamental units *length L, time T,* and *density D,* then *volume L³* becomes a derived unit ; and *mass M* is defined as the product of volume x density ; $M = V x D$.

Coming now to a more complex problem concerning the primary aspects of matter, Newton distinguished between matter and weight. The amount of motion is due to an inherent property of body—a property different from weight ; that property he called mass. Under certain conditions, for Newton the mass of a body may be measured by its weight.[2] In the second edition of the *Principia* in 1713, Roger Cotes [3] stated in the

[1] *The Science of Mechanics,* translated by McCormack, Chicago, 1907, p. 194.

[2] *Principia*, vol. i, pp. 1–2.

[3] Cotes edited and revised this edition under the direct supervision of Newton himself.

Preface that, because gravity is actually observed to be universally true of all bodies, therefore we assume that gravity is a primary quality of bodies, just as much as extension, mobility, impenetrability. Explaining this statement to Clarke,[1] Newton stated that it was not his intention to assert gravity to be one of the qualities of matter, but rather to point out his ignorance as to the actual properties of matter, of which, it may be, gravity is one. But Newton is not altogether neutral as to the question of gravity being a quality of matter, as we may gather from his addition to the *regulae philosophandi*,[2] wherein he said that the universal qualities of matter are extension, hardness, impenetrability, mobility, and inertia. The above suggestion of Cotes is altogether ignored by Newton in his added question to the new edition of the *Optics* of 1717.

The term density as used in the definition of matter was never defined by Newton, but from what he said elsewhere we may judge that he thought the smallest hard and simple particles to be equally dense, and that the density of any mass is proportional to the number and size of its particles in a given space.

[1] Edleston, *Corr.*, pp. 158–9.
[2] Third Rule. See also Newton's advertisement to the second edition of *Optics*, 1717.

Newton was familiar with the experiments of Boyle in regard to density. Newton came to believe that density is a primary quality of matter. The density of gas of a given temperature is proportional to the volume it occupies, while the gas remains always the same. That constant factor, in the experiments of Boyle, Newton called the quantity of matter or mass of the gas. To make this vague idea scientifically useful he gave it a scientific definition, verifying it by nature. Matter or mass was defined by Newton as being proportional to volume and density. Boyle's experimental results showed $PV = $ constant—only for ideal gasses however. The definition of force like that of matter had a scientific meaning given it. Movement was associated with force, which was defined as a moving secondary cause. But the concept of force assumed a mathematical meaning at the hands of Newton. This mathematical concept called force was put at the basis of mechanics and was centred around the quantity of movement. The object of Newton was to be able to measure accurately mass and force.

It was Galileo who gave Newton the idea of force. Galileo's experiments showed that a force acting on falling body equals its mass multiplied by a quantity which is constant, and that this is true of all bodies. Newton knowing this, and seeing its importance from his own hypothesis of gravity, began to experiment still further by the use of a pendulum. He concluded from these experiments that the period of oscillation of a pendulum measures the ratio of the weight of a body to its mass, deducing the exact formula, and proving that if this ratio of weight to mass is constant then the period of oscillation of any one pendulum is the same for any amplitude of vibration so long as it is small compared with the length of the pendulum thread, and that the square of the period of oscillation is proportional to the length of the pendulum. Newton also proved, for a series of different materials, that the ratio of the weight and mass of all bodies is the same.

These concepts of forces, which Newton developed after Galileo, can best be understood if we imagine the forces passing through the centres of bodies, and if we attribute to these centres mathematical properties. An expression of forces in mathematical terms is a useful scientific concept to express movements, which are called the causes of these movements. As Newton says : it is by analogy of muscular effort that we get the mechanical notion of force.[1] Newton regarded these forces as results of shocks, pressures, and

[1] *Principia*, Def. V, p. 4.

as of centripetal nature.[1] All forces are homogeneous for Newton ; one type is equal to another.
The unity of forces becomes a fundamental principle of Newton's physics.

Descartes, Malebranche, Fontenelle, and Huygens, on the contrary, deduced the forces of
weight, or the planetary gravitation, from a
certain disposition of matter in the world. To
them the Newtonian gravitational explanation
based upon ' attraction ' was obscure and ques-
tionable, while that of Descartes's was based upon
clear mechanical principles which were acknow-
ledged by almost everybody. Matter for the
Cartesians was pure extension, and differs in
places by its thinness or thickness of structure.
Descartes explained weight as a consequence of the
pressure of the whirling bodies against the parts
of space, in which they are pressed against the
heavenly bodies, or, if not, they are kept in close
proximity to them. This notion of weight is not
hard to arrive at in a rationalist's metaphysics,
where matter is pure extension, and its individuality is due to form only. In that geometric
universe nothing exists but extension and move--
ment ; and from this Descartes wanted to
explain or deduce forces as the causes of motion.
Naturally it was necessary that these forces

[1] *Principia*, Def. iv, p. 5.

should have been born under special circumstances, applied in special configuration ; and as a consequence of that they would have to be complex and not elementary. Gravitation, therefore, is not a universal law, Descartes thought, because it exists only in certain types and parts of matter. That is, Descartes's theory presupposed two kinds of bodies, the one gravitating in the ratio to the quantity of matter, and the other in the ratio of shape, &c., of greatness or smallness. According to the variations of respective configurations of the bodies, he believed they could transform themselves, one into the other, acquiring or losing mass without acquiring or losing matter. In fact, if Descartes admits weight to be due to the shape, or pure extension, then it necessarily follows that weight changes with the shape or figure of the particles. It was this conception which had been experimentally disproved by Newton.

As we have seen above, Descartes thought of mass as independent of force ; he thought it necessary to have recourse to an efficient cause in order to explain the action of the forces. The nature of movement was explained by Descartes as this efficient cause, which is God ; God who is perfect, simple, and immutable, is responsible for the simplicity and the conservation of movement.

Newton, on the contrary, defined mass in terms of force, and *vice versa*. As is clear now, from a previous discussion,[1] Newton's idea of force and mass made these concepts only secondary causes—scientific definitions, and not ultimate and metaphysical ones, as they were conceived by Descartes. The nature of force, of mass, and of motion, was, for Newton, only functionally connected with the mathematical laws of mass and force. The motion of mass is only conceivable through the observation of a field of constant forces, and the conception of force is inseparable from the idea of mass and acceleration. These facts once obtained by experiment and mathematically expressed constitute the positive basis for mechanics. Efficient or metaphysical causes are not necessary considerations for the science of mechanics.

To summarize Newton's doctrine of atoms, we may say that he regarded atoms, or, as he called them, particles or corpuscles, as hard or undivided, impenetrable, possessing extension and density, mobility, and inertia. The size of the corpuscles is responsible for their colour ; according to their different colours the atoms are of varying sizes and irregularities of figure. Any aggregate of them is called a mass, and is necessarily measured

[1] See above, Chapter II, sect. i.   See also Chapter V.

by its density and volume or bulk. The weight
of such a mass depends upon the physical properties of matter, independent of the forms or figure
of the particles and of the bulk. Weight conveys
the idea of force, which is conceived through
the analogy of muscular exertion. Force and
mass were, for Newton, scientific concepts, expressing properties of nature. Force, however, is
not a primary attribute of matter, Newton thought,
but on the contrary, matter is inert, but mobile.

Newton's discussion as analysed thus far raised
the following problem : If particles have the
quality of mobility and inertia, what is responsible
for their motion ? Newton's principle of inertia
does not account for motion,[1] but only for per-
sistence. Since Newton did not agree with
Descartes that one of the qualities of matter is
motion, as discussed above, and threw overboard
Descartes's theory of vortices, then he had a
further problem—metaphysical rather than mathematical—on his hand, namely, how are movement
and attraction made possible ? What started
matter moving ? What makes particles of matter
attract each other ? There must, said Newton, like
Gassendi, be some other primary principle which
is the cause and the conserver of this motion.[2]

[1] *Optics*, 3rd ed., pp. 372 ff. ; *Principia*, vol. iii, p. 4.
[2] *Optics*, p. 373.

Let us come back to the questions raised above and ask : What is the ' real ' cause of motion ? What is the cause of the attraction between particles of matter ? Newton never claimed that the mathematical formulation of force is the real metaphysical or ultimate and underlying cause of motion.[1] It is only a scientific description of movement and not an explanation ; it is the *how* and not the *why* of things. Nor did he claim that the centripetal forces acting at a distance are the fundamental or primary cause or an explanation of gravity. Newton, like all the men of his day, considered it absurd to think of attraction as actually taking place between bodies *at a distance, without any intervening medium.* As Clarke, whom Newton accepted as his advocate,[2] said, ' That one body should attract another without any intermediate means, is indeed not a miracle, but a contradiction. For it is supposing something to act where it is not.' [3]

Newton has shown that force is always a part of a stress, and that it is always produced by the action of two particles of matter upon each other ; it is of interest to know—if bodies do not act at a distance—what is the mechanism or method by

---

[1] *Optics*, 3rd ed., pp. 372–3 ; *Principia*, vol. iii, p. 4.
[2] See above, Chapter IV, sect. i.
[3] Leibniz and Clarke, *Correspondence*, p. 51.

which one particle may act upon another, or
what is the mechanism by which each and every
particle may attract and be attracted mutually
by the sun and by the earth ? Naturally, from
analogy of everyday behaviour, we think that
there must be some medium by means of which
the action and reaction is made possible. But
in the case of Newton we find him at first
hostile to the idea of an all-pervading corporeal
ether, which would make such an analogy intelligible.[1]

As he said in 1675, about ten years before the
publication of his *Principia* : ' But for this end
I must first . . . cast out what he [Hook] has
borrowed from Descartes and others, viz., that
there is an ethereal medium ; that light is the
action of this medium ; that it is less implicated
in the parts of solid bodies, and so moves freely in
them and transmits light more readily through
them. . . . This, I think, is, in short, the
sum of his hypothesis, and in all this I have
nothing in common with him. . . .'[2] And Dr.
J. C. Gregory possesses a manuscript written
by Newton in 1702, in which Newton literally

[1] See above, Chapter III.
[2] Newton to Oldenburg, 21 December 1675, found in S. J.
Rigaud's *Correspondence of Scientific Men of the Seventeenth
Century,* vol. ii, p. 378, Oxford, 1841.

and explicitly rejects the ether theory as merely guessing.[1]

Then how shall we describe attraction of bodies, if we refute both notions, that of the all-pervading ether of Descartes—the conception apparently necessary for belief in motion by impact—and that of action at a distance ?

As part of his answer, Newton turned to mathematics, attempting, in this phase of his reply, to explain the *how* rather from the descriptive than from the metaphysical point of view. The notion of Newton that the forces of gravity of the earth are the sum of the forces of each and every one of its particles made it possible for him to conceive that all terrestrial bodies attract each other, and furthermore, that each particle in the universe attracts every other. And by conceiving particles as mathematical points, and bodies as the sum-resultant of these particles, then solids, mathematically considered, are the sums of points. Also, the movement or the force of attraction of a body is in the same ratio to the movement or force of attraction of its particles as the movements and the force of attraction of a mathematical solid are to the movement and the force of attraction of its points. And for mathematical or scientific purposes Newton con-

[1] Brewster's *Life of Sir Isaac Newton*, 1st ed., London, 1840, ii. 302–5.

ceived the force of a solid mass as the force of a single point in the centre of the solid [1] because a homogeneous sphere attracts as if its mass were concentrated at its centre. By so conceiving mathematical spheres—a conception possible because God guarantees the regularity and geometricity of the world [2]—Newton thought that he was able to demonstrate that the attraction between them would be as if every particle of matter should attract every other particle with a force directly proportional to the mass of each, and to the inverse square of their distances. To put it in another way, when the distance between two particles which attract or repel one another changes, the stress between these particles changes also, its change varying according to the direct product of its masses and inversely as the square of the distances between them ; hence, the force which the corpuscles exert upon each other is $F = \dfrac{mm'}{d^2}$ or $F = G\dfrac{mm'}{d^2}$, where F = force, m = mass, d = distance, and G = constant. As Newton said : Two principal cases of attraction are, first, ' when the centripetal forces [3] decrease in a duplicate ratio of the distances ', and secondly, when they

---

[1] *Principia*, vol. i, pp. 262, 264, 293–6, 298–9 ; vol. ii, pp. 236, 387.

[2] *Ibid.*, p. 379, and Gen. Schol. ; *Optics*, 3rd ed., Qu. 31.

[3] Newton defines centripetal force as ' that by which bodies are drawn or impelled, or any way tend, towards a point as to

increase in a simple ratio of the distances ; causing
the bodies in both cases to revolve in conic
sections, and ' composing spherical bodies whose
centripetal forces observe the same law of increase
or decrease in the recess from the centre as the
forces of the particles themselves do ; which is
very remarkable '.[1]   From this rule, it follows
that when any point or any sphere, which really
is regarded only as a point of centripetal force,
moves according to the above rule of inverse
squares and with a velocity not too high, then its
path of revolution would be an ellipse. That was
the reason why Newton could at once answer
the query of Halley, when he was asked to describe the curve that a particle would describe if it
should move in accordance with the above law.
By substituting a constant for the mathematical
point, and bodies for the mathematical spheres,
Newton was surprised to find the correspondence
astronomically correct.

As a result of this substitution, the following
results were evident : (1) Kepler's second law
proves that the action of force upon each planet
is towards a centre of force, for instance, the sun.

a centre.' (*Math. Princ. of Nat. Philos.*, Book I, American ed.,
Def. 5, vol. i, p. 4).

[1] *Principia*, vol. i, p. 278 ; Book I, Sect. xii, Prop. 78,
Scholium.

(2) Kepler's first law proves that this centripetal force diminishes proportionally as the increase of the square of the distances. (3) Kepler's third law proves that the same kind of force acts upon all the planets, in the proportion to the mass of the sun. (4) The force acting on the moon or the satellites depends upon the mass of their central body. (5) By knowing the distance of any planet from the sun and the length of the orbit described by that planet, we may determine the mass of the sun, which is the central body of the planets. And many other deductions follow from the above substitutions.[1]

Newton's mathematical description of the cosmos was simple, and could lend itself to a more definite treatment than any complex ether-hypothesis. Newton did not wish to miss the advantages of the simplicity of the conception of centripetal forces by assuming some highly fictitious ethereal mechanism.

But Newton, however, does not rest with his mathematical treatment of gravity ; he at times does suggest an explanation of motion by assuming the existence of an all-pervading ether. In the next chapter we shall discuss Newton's suggestions of an ether hypothesis as a means to explain physically or mechanically the motion of bodies.

[1] Mach, E., *Science of Mechanics*, Chicago, 1907, pp. 187–9.

III

NEWTON'S PHYSICAL DOCTRINE OF GRAVITY

§ I

NEWTON felt that his mathematical expression
of gravity was not a final explanation of celestial
motion, but rather a descriptive empirical law;
he, however, suggested a possible physical explanation, and, at the same time, another explanation which is not physical. These two opposing
suggestions we will now discuss historically in
order to determine their significance and meaning.
As it happens that these two suggestions are very
closely related it will be impossible always to
discuss them separately.

In the first Latin edition of the *Optics* in 1706,
Newton pointed hypothetically to the possibility
of the existence of ether. He stated, in the twenty-
eighth query, that he emphatically objected to
the doctrine of a fluid medium which fills the
heavens, unless it be an ' exceeding rare ' one,
because of the regular and lasting movements of
the planets and comets. It follows from this that
the heavens are free of all ' sensible resistance ',
therefore of all ' sensible matter ', except that
perhaps some parts of it may contain very thin

vapours, steams, or effluvia, ' arising from the atmosphere of the earth, planets, and comets ', and of an exceedingly rare ethereal medium. Although his position regarding ether, as taken up previous to the republication of his *Optics* of 1706, is largely unchanged, he conceded to ether a more definite status. Newton, in his advertisement to the second English edition of his *Optics* in 1717, stated that, because he does not believe gravity to be an essential property of bodies, he will add one question concerning the cause of gravity, putting it in the form of a question because he is ' not yet satisfied about it, for want of Experiments '.

Newton points to the possibility of the existence of ether, because, if we should suspend two thermometers in two perfectly airtight vessels, so that they might not touch the vessels, withdrawing ' all ' the air from one of the vessels, so that there would be a vacuum, while the other would contain air, we should notice that the temperature registered on the enclosed thermometers would at each moment be the same, no matter how we vary the temperature of the room containing both vessels. Therefore Newton asked whether the heat of the warm room is not conveyed through a very rare medium ? Is not this rare medium the same as that medium by which light is transmitted, and by whose vibrations light communicates heat to the bodies, and is put into ' fits ' of easy reflection and easy transmission ? Is not this rare medium very elastic, and therefore expanded through the heavens, readily pervading all bodies ? [1] Is not the different density in different places of this rare medium responsible for the refraction of light, light receding always from the denser to the rarer parts of the mediums ? And furthermore, may we not say that this medium is rarest in solid bodies and most dense in vacuums ? Because light, passing through a glass, and falling obliquely upon the farthest surface thereof, is completely reflected, this proceeding rather from the ' density and vigour ' of the medium ' without and beyond the glass than from the rarity and weakness thereof '.[2] Does not this ether, by passing out of dense reflective objects into vacuum, become gradually denser, so that, when it refracts the rays of light, it bends them gradually into curved lines ? And is it not because of this condensation of the medium that, when it passes beyond the body, it thereby causes the *inflexions* of the rays of light, ' which pass by the edges of dense bodies ' at some distance from them ? [3]

[1] Qu. 18 (*Optics*, 3rd ed., 1721, pp. 323–4).
[2] Qu. 19 (*Optics*, 3rd ed., 1721, p. 324).
[3] Qu. 20 (*Optics*, 3rd ed., 1721, p. 324).

And, furthermore, Newton continued, is not this medium most rare within the great and dense bodies, that is, the sun, stars, planets, and the comets, more so than it is in the space surrounding them ; and does it not become more and more dense as it leaves the surrounding spaces of the bodies ? Is not this medium, most rare at the layer immediately adjoining the surface of the sun, becoming gradually and perpetually more and more dense as the distance from the sun becomes greater ; that is, would it not be very dense beyond the planet Saturn, while very rare near the sun ? And, if this be so, may we not say that this difference of density is the cause of gravity, every body endeavouring to move towards the rarer medium ? 'And though this increase of density may at great distances be exceedingly slow, yet, if the elastic force of this medium be exceedingly great, it may suffice to impel Bodies from the denser parts of the Medium towards the rarer, with all that power which we call Gravity.' We may gather, from the rapidity of ethereal vibrations, that is, movement of sound, that this medium is really exceedingly elastic.[1]

As we know that magnetic attraction is proportional inversely to mass, being greater in small

[1] Qu. 21 (*Optics*, 3rd ed., 1721, p. 325).

magnets than in greater ones,[1] so also, Newton says, gravity is proportionally greater in surfaces of small planets than those of greater ones, and small bodies are also more agitated by electric attraction than greater ones are ; so ' the smallness of the rays of light may contribute very much to the power of the agent by which they are refracted. And so if any one should suppose that ether (like our air) may contain particles which endeavour to recede from one another (for I do not know what this ether is), and that its particles are exceedingly smaller than those of air, or even than those of light : The exceeding smallness of its particles may contribute to the greatness of the force by which these particles may recede from one another, and thereby make that medium exceedingly more rare and elastic than air, and by consequence exceedingly less able to resist the motion of projectiles, and exceedingly more able to press upon gross bodies, by endeavouring to expand itself.' [2]

May it not be said that the planets, comets, and all large bodies move more freely and with less resistance in this ethereal medium than in any fluid, this medium filling all space without leaving any pores, and therefore being denser

---

[1] *Optics*, 3rd ed., 1721, p. 326.
[2] Qu. 21 (*Optics*, 3rd ed., 1721, pp. 326–7).

than quicksilver or gold? Newton further questions.[1]

Especially in this last query, it may be noted in passing, that the ether, which Newton only tentatively suggests, is different from the Cartesian one in all its main aspects. Descartes's ether is uniformly distributed, pervading all space equally, and being in constant agitation, whereas the medium that Newton had in mind is of different degrees of rareness in different places; it is elastic; its elasticity is proportional to the density of the medium; it is composed of parts with empty spaces between them—so we have still a vacuum, although in less amount—and it is inert. Newton did speak of ether as possessing 'vigour', by which he meant pressure, but he did not think of it as a cause of the movement of particles.[2]

In the third English edition of the *Optics*, 1721, Newton again asked if vision be not chiefly performed by the vibration of a rare medium, which is excited in the bottom of the eye by the rays of light; and whether hearing be not due to the vibrations of this ether or some other medium, excited in the auditory nerves by the 'tremors of the air'—both types of vibrations being conducted

[1] Qu. 22 (*Optics*, 3rd. ed., 1721, p. 327); also Qu. 28 (3rd ed., 1721, p. 343).

[2] Below we shall deal with this question of 'vigour' more fully.

through the nerves 'into the place of sensation'. And may we not say much the same about any or all the other sensations ? [1] And may we not suppose that 'animal motion' if performed by the vibrations of that medium, 'excited in the Brain by the power of the will, and propagated from thence through the solid, pellucid, and uniform capillamenta of the nerves into the muscles, for contracting and dilating them' ? [2]

In the queries quoted immediately above, Newton seems to suggest an explanation for the reaction of nerve-current and animal motion in terms of ether vibrations.

From the above-quoted questions some students of Newton supposed that he changed from his initial position—action at a distance—as stated in the first editions of his works, to the hypothesis of ether as a mechanical medium which is the cause of acceleration between bodies.

Mabilleau put it as follows : 'A la vérité, Newton fut effrayé de ce concert d'objections, et il tenta d'abord, en 1717, (les critiques précédentes de Leibniz sont de 1716) dans la préface de la seconde édition de l'Optique, de démentir toute interprétation philosophique de la théorie : " hypotheses non fingo ". Mais auparavant déjà,

---

[1] *Optics*, 3rd ed., London, 1721 ; Qu. 23, p. 328.
[2] *Ibid.*, Qu. 24.

(en 1704, dans l'Optique) devant l'insistance de
ses disciples, il avait bien fallu qu'il proposât un
système plausible, acceptable pour les savants.
Il s'était tiré d'affaire en revenant catégorique-
ment au mécanisme : l'univers, selon lui, est
rempli de matière éthérée, de densité differente
selon les régions. L'éther est invisible, mais actif,
élastique ; il pénètre tous les corps et il réside
entre leurs particules. C'est sans doute le ressort
de cet élément, qui, agissant sur les masses
physiques par pression, et les poussant des places
les plus denses vers les plus rares, produit leur
gravitation mutuelle : " omnibus nimirum corporibus, qua parte medium densius est, ex ea
parte recedere conatibus in partes rariores "
(*Optics*, Lib. III, Quaest. 21.) ' [1]

Mabilleau's reference to Leibniz deals with the
accusation made by Leibniz in 1710, that Newton
employed ' occult powers ' in order to explain the
cause of gravitation.   In order to understand the
accusation, it may be well first to state Newton's
suggestions to which Leibniz objected ;   and
secondly, Leibnizian dynamics, in order to see
what kind of explanation of motion Leibniz
regarded as scientific.

As we have stated in the beginning of the
chapter, Newton seemed to fluctuate between two

[1] Mabilleau, *Histoire de la Philosophie Atomistique*, p. 443.

positions : about the time the reader of the
third edition of the *Optics* thinks himself secure in
the idea that Newton seeks the explanation of
motion in the ethereal medium, he finds this idea
undermined by the very last query.[1] In this
query Newton asked : ' Have not the small
Particles of Bodies certain Powers, Virtues, or
Forces, by which they act at a distance, not only
upon the Rays of Light for reflecting, refracting
and inspecting them,[2] but upon one another for
producing a great part of the Phenomena of
Nature ? For it's well known that Bodies act
one upon another by the Attraction of Gravity,
Magnetism, and Electricity ; and these Instances
show the Tenor and Course of Nature, and make it
not improbable but that there may be more
attractive Power than these. For Nature is very
consonant and conformable to herself.[3] How these
attractions may be perform'd I do not here consider. What I call Attraction may be perform'd
by impulse, or by some other means unknown to
me. I use that Word here to signify only in
general any Force by which Bodies tend towards
one another, whatsoever be the Cause. For we

[1] *Optics*, 3rd ed., London, 1721, Qu. 31, p. 350.

[2] Newton develops this idea more fully in the *Optics*, 3rd ed.,
Qu. 31, p. 349.

[3] The spirit of this question is the same as found in his
first edition of the *Principia* especially in the General Scholia.

must learn from the Phaenomena of Nature what Bodies attract one another, and what are the Laws and Properties of the Attraction, before we enquire the Cause by which Attraction is perform'd. The Attraction of Gravity, Magnetism, and Electricity, reach to very sensible distances, and so have been observed by vulgar Eyes, and there may be others which reach to so small distances as hitherto escape Observation; and perhaps electrical Attraction may reach to such small distances, even without being excited by Friction.[1] '

Just as Newton, when invoking the ether hypothesis to explain motion, applied this hypothesis not only in the realm of pure physics, but in chemistry and physiology, so Newton, when temporarily abandoning the ether theory for the theory of ' forces ', applied that theory too in several fields. Thus, he used it in the following experiments, conceiving the possibility of explaining through ' forces ' chemical reactions and compounds due to attraction. For example, when one pours ' aqua fortis, or spirit of vitriol ' upon filings of iron, the iron is dissolved in the acid, giving off a great amount of heat and ' ebullition '. Newton appears to believe that this heat and ebullition are due to the violent

[1] *Optics*, 3rd ed., London, 1721, Qu. 31, pp. 350–1.

motion of parts, and that it follows that the acid parts rush towards the parts of iron with great violence, and, running forcibly into the pores of iron, until they get in between the particles thereof, completely surround them, by which action they loosen them, setting them at liberty to float off in the acid. And furthermore, he asks, do not the acid particles when distilled give rise to some heat, but would they not separate from the iron particles without giving rise to very violent heat, and is not this a confirmation of the possibility that attraction actually takes place between them ? [1]

When we dissolve a very small quantity of salt or vitriol in a very large quantity of water the salt or vitriol will dissolve evenly throughout the solvent. May not the above phenomenon imply, Newton reasons, that ' the parts of salt or vitriol recede from one another, and endeavour to expand themselves, and get as far asunder as the quantity of water in which they float will allow ? And does not this Endeavour imply that they have a repulsive Force by which they fly from one another, or at least, that they attract the water more strongly than they do one another ? For as all things ascend in water, which are less attracted than water by the gravitating Power

[1] *Optics*, 3rd ed., London, 1721, Qu. 31, pp. 352-3.

of the Earth ; so all the Particles of Salt which float in Water, and are less attracted than water by any one Particle of Salt, must recede from that Particles, and give way to the more attracted water.' [1]

Newton also asked if the combination or cohesion of hard atoms or particles is not due to some force of attraction which is very strong when atoms come together, and by virtue of this great strength keeps them together ? For it is difficult to conceive how such very hard particles, when they lie together and touch only at few points, could stick together so firmly ' without the assistance of something which causes them to be attracted or pressed toward one another '. [2]

As a matter of fact, it has been experimentally determined (by Hawksby) that the attraction is ' almost reciprocally in a duplicate proportion of the distance of the middle of the drop from the Concourse of the Glasses [two plane polished plates of glass, three inches broad by twenty inches long, are laid so that one of them is parallel to the horizon, while the other lies upon the first so that at one of their ends they touch one another and make an angle of about ten or fifteen minutes], viz. reciprocally in a simple proportion, by reason of the spreading of the drop, and its touching of

[1] *Ibid.*, pp. 362–3.　　　[2] *Ibid.*, pp. 364–5.

the glass in a larger surface ; and again reciprocally in a simple proportion, by reason of the
attractions growing stronger within the same
quantity of attracting surfaces.' Therefore the
attraction within the same quantity of attracting
surface ' is reciprocally as the distance between
the glasses '. Consequently, where the distance
is very small the attraction is exceedingly great.[1]

It was to the above-stated suggestions by
Newton that Leibniz objected. He felt that
Newton's use of forces—acting at a distance—to
explain attraction was not scientific. Leibniz
thought that his own dynamics did away with any
assumption in any sense ' occult '.

Leibniz divided the qualities of matter into
primary (i. e. extension, which is essentially
passive) and secondary matter (the quality of
which concerns dynamics—which is endowed with
force). To follow the dynamics of Leibniz we
shall show the relations of his work to that of
Descartes and Newton. There was a tendency
of the time to explain movement through the
existence of ether. And Newton later on did
admit ether, especially in his explanation of light.
He showed, however, that this ether is thinly
spread out, like light itself, and that the resistance
which it offers to celestial bodies is negligible.

[1] *Optics*, 3rd ed., London, 1721, pp. 368–9.

It is not like Descartes's matter, which fills all space, and under all conditions must develop great resistance. But Newton had a still stronger reason to argue against Descartes. Let us try to explain this reason. If we would reduce all physical forces to movements of matter as the fundamental cause we must, in order to assure the continuance of the universe, assume the continuity and indestructibility of motion.[1] The trouble with Descartes was that his reason for the continuity of movement was logical and not physical. Descartes held that the essence of matter is extension, that the quantity of motion in the universe is constant, and that the force is proportioned to the quantity of matter; while Leibniz wanted to prove that the essence of matter is not really extension, and that the total quantity of motion is not constant, but that the quantity of motion in any given direction is constant. He also believed that dynamics must develop an ultimate concept which is force, and that that force is an activity which is essential to secondary substance. As Russell [2] points out: ' The doctrine of force is closely connected with every

---

[1] The Epicureans claimed the indestructibility of motion because they could explain the continuity of life in no other way.

[2] *A Critical Exposition of the Philosophy of Leibniz with Appendix of Leading Passages*, Cambridge, 1900, p. 81.

part of contingent truths, with the conception of substance as the source of all its predicates, with the plurality of independent causal series, with the physical nature of all substances, and with the whole theory of activity, liberty, and determination'; that is, force is prior to extension and the true grounds for inferring the plurality of substances. As Leibniz put it, ' We have elsewhere suggested that there is in corporeal things something besides extension, nay, prior to extension, namely, the force of nature everywhere implanted by its Author.' [1]

Impact was the accepted form of dynamic interaction. Newtonian gravitation, action at a distance, Leibniz rejected, claiming that only the assumption of some ' occult power ' could make such an action possible without the assumption of an all-pervading fluid. Leibniz was not able to see clearly that there are really three possible dynamical and mechanical explanations of motion: first, the Newtonian one—the doctrine of unextended centres of force which operate at a distance ; second, the existence of hard extended atoms operating by means of impact ; third, the existence

[1] *New Essays Concerning Human Understanding*, by J. W. Leibniz, &c., London, 1896, p. 671, and *Leibnizens Mathematischen Schriften*, herausgegeben von C. F. Gerhardt, 1850–63, Part VI, p. 235.

of an all-pervading fluid, of which the modern doctrine of ether, as employed in the theory of
electricity, may be used as an example. Leibniz,
however, took the view that impact is most fundamental, and with that he should have taken the
theory of extended atoms of Gassendi and Huygens.
And again, his belief in an ether should have led
him to the third possibility, while his acceptance
of spaces being relative and of the plurality of
unextended atoms, if logically developed, should
have forced him to something like Newton's
position concerning action at a distance. As
Russell points out, Leibniz's dynamics is only a
mass of confusion. The true Leibnizian dynamics
is that of Boscovich.[1] This theory is a simple
development of the Newtonian dynamics, in
which all matter consists of material points, and
all action is action at a distance. These material
points are unextended like the monads, to which
Boscovich refers as analogous,[2] and in order to
preserve their mutual independence it is only
necessary to regard the attraction or repulsion
as due to the perception of one monad by the
other, which, as a matter of fact, Leibniz actually
does.[3] Russell believes that the reason Leibniz

---

[1] *Theoria Philosophiae Naturalis*, see especially Part I,
§ 138.   [3] Venetian ed., 1763, p. xxv.
[2] Boscovich differs from Newton chiefly in assuming that,

did not follow up the lead of Newton as did Boscovich, Kant, and Lotze, which would have been only natural for him to do, is that in later life he quarrelled with Newton concerning the calculus and ' he did not choose to admit that Newton had anything to teach him '. Guhrauer [1] suggests that Leibniz never took the trouble to read the *Principia*. But that could not have been the main reason, Russell thinks,[2] why Leibniz rejected action at a distance. The *Principia* was published in 1687, and Leibniz had developed his philosophy and dynamics before that time. Leibniz rejected Newton's position in regard to the existence of atoms, vacuum, and action at a distance. His objection to the first two have been discussed in the second part of the first chapter. Russell thinks that the Leibnizian objection to the last one was nothing but prejudice.[3] There is no reason, Russell says, why monads, which do not in any case interact, cannot see within them the actions which take place at a distance, and that should be just as much a cause for action as that

at very small distances, the force between two particles is repulsive. He also differs from Newton in regarding action at a distance as ultimate.

[1] *Leibniz Eine Biographie*, vol. i, p. 279.

[2] Russell, *A Critical Exposition of the Philosophy of Leibniz, with Appendix of Leading Passages*, Cambridge, 1900, p. 91.

[3] Russell, *op. cit.*, p. 93.

which takes place near them (impact). ' There seems to be no metaphysical reason, and in the time of Newton no dynamical reason, for such a rejection.'

If we are to suppose that Leibniz did not accept Newton's contributions to dynamics because Leibniz wrote his dynamics before he knew of Newton's conclusions, as Russell believes,[1] it would be very hard to explain the fact that Leibniz asked Newton to correspond with him concerning what Leibniz called Newton's ' use of occult powers ', a challenge taken up by one of Newton's ablest defenders, Samuel Clarke.[2] Clarke, in defending Newton, denied the use of any ' occult powers ', and also denied the existence of a rare ether.[3] Newton himself, in the third edition of his *Optics*, speaking about the cause of movement of particles, said that there are certain active principles, such as that of gravity, &c., but that these principles are not ' occult qualities ', but rather general laws of nature by which things are formed.[4] The reason for the dispute seems to

[1] Russell believes, furthermore, that another reason why Leibniz did not accept Newton's contributions to dynamics was of ' vulgar prejudice ' as pointed out above.

[2] Brewster's *Memoirs*, &c., vol. ii, p. 378.

[3] Leibniz and Clarke correspondence, especially Clarke's fourth reply.

[4] *Optics*, Qu. 31 ; see also the unsigned preface, written by

us to have been of a more fundamental nature than Russell supposes. This reason may become clearer when we discuss the conflict between Huygens and Newton, since Huygens had influenced Leibniz especially with regard to the above dispute.

Huygens was an opponent of Newton's theories of light and gravity. Democritus, giving no explanation for his ideas, had told the world that atoms possess gravity. The Platonists of Huygens's time believed gravitational motion due to a spiritual force, which is immaterial, operating by means of emanations. This last explanation of gravity was abhorrent to Huygens, who asked how something immaterial could act upon material substance ? Descartes claimed that the explanation was to be found in physics and that we need not go beyond physics. The explanation, he said, lies in the nature of bodies and their movements. Huygens's hypothesis of gravity presupposed the existence of ether, hard atoms, and Cartesian vortices.[1] Huygens later admitted the correctness of Newtonian mathematical deductions,[2] forsaking Descartes's theory of the

Newton, to the *Commercium Epistolicum* (Brewster's *Memoirs*, p. 378).

[1] *Dissertatio de causa gravitatis*, *Opera Reliqua*, 1728, vol. i, pp. 101–2.

[2] *Additamentum*, pp. 116 ff.

vortices, but he would not agree with Newton's hypothesis of the mutual attraction of the parts of the masses, because Newton could not explain it by mechanical means, nor does it logically follow from his laws of motion. Huygens did not object to the Newtonian hypothesis of centripetal forces ; in fact Huygens as well as Leibniz himself postulated such forces, and, furthermore, Huygens even accepted Newton's mathematical deductions. Leibniz himself thought that every piece of matter has its own force, and is the source of all change ; as he claimed, every object is really moved, not by other bodies, but by its own force [1]—force bears the same relation to matter as Aristotelian form does. It is this force, thought Leibniz, which is the *entelechy*, analogous to a soul which constitutes the object's individuality, and its nature follows a perpetual law pre-established by God, which is responsible for all changes taking place spontaneously. Force is a certain condition of things ; it is the law according to which the universe unfolds or develops. But even here Leibniz made a distinction in the idea of force, one being primary and always constant, and the other (with which dynamics is concerned) derivative. This force is transferred from body

[1] *The Philosophical Works of Leibniz*, p. 124, and *Die Philosophischen Schriften*, vol. iv, p. 515.

to body by impact. So all things in a plenum are connected.[1]

Huygens felt, as did Leibniz, that the real, final, and metaphysical explanation of gravity is to be found in force ; Huygens accepted Newtonian centripetal forces, while Leibniz identified force with the inherent universal law by which matter or the monads change in accordance with a definite plan. The Leibnizian notion of force is closely connected with law ; force is a certain condition of things or substance [2] which brings about change. Force, as mathematically expressed, was not regarded by Newton as it was by Leibniz, as a metaphysical or final explanation of gravity. As Newton expresses it, these forces or ' principle are not occult qualities of nature ' ; we must find the laws first ' before we may speak about their causes ' (i. e. of attraction).[3] But Leibniz took Newton's empirical laws—scientific expressions or descriptions in mathematical terms of what actually takes place in nature—as metaphysical explanations of gravity. Of course any one

[1] *Die Philosophischen Schriften*, vol. ii, p. 112.

[2] Leibnizian use of the word ; ' substance ' is not equivalent to matter but to the ' real ' or the substratum as used by Spinoza.

[3] *Optics*, 3rd ed., London, 1721, Qu. 30, p. 351 ; Qu. 31. The same ideas are to be found in Newton's first edition of his *Principia*.

looking for the centripetal forces to attract bodies actually at a distance would think of this attraction as if some occult powers were in operation, but, as a matter of fact, Newton did not aim to explain the causes of gravity when he developed his mathematical law. Huygens felt that in order to describe gravity in terms of centripetal forces one must couple it with a mechanical explanation, through the admission of an ether hypothesis, and not, as Newton did, in terms of attracting forces acting at a distance. Leibniz had no need for the doctrines of action at a distance, because change and motion in his system, from the primary point of view, took place according to a pre-established harmony within the bodies spontaneously. He thought that it was only in the derivative sense that motion is the result of the transfer of force from one body to another, and this takes place by impact. Newton, however, thought of centripetal forces mathematically expressed, acting at a distance, as we have said, as a natural law, as a scientific description of natural relations expressed in mathematical terms. Action at a distance, or physical attraction, was for Newton not a metaphysical explanation of the cause of motion. It was because Leibniz and Huygens never made the distinction between physical or mathematical descriptions of natural relations and the explanatory causes of philosophy in general or theology, which was a fundamental part of Newton's natural philosophy, that they could never understand Newton. A mathematical expression or an expression in experimental philosophy, Newton felt, deals with physical relationships or the laws which are in nature, while the primary notions of philosophy in general deal with the underlying ('substratum') or the 'real' and 'ultimate' causes of nature. It was because Newton did not identify the mechanical or secondary causes with theological or primary causes, and because he sought for the real cause of gravitation outside of the realm of physics, that he was accused by Leibniz of the use of 'occult powers'. Furthermore, while centripetal forces acting at a distance offered a good mathematical explanation, Newton himself did not believe that forces actually operate at a distance. Neither Leibniz nor Huygens, however, could see the significance of such a mathematical description.

Newton thought that all planetary action is by impact, as all other motion, and it was necessary to admit a centre of intervention, but this centre of intervention was not accessible experimentally. However, it was not necessary to admit the existence of ether *a priori*, but, in spite of that, forces acting at a distance without the assumption of some intervening medium could not be rationally conceived. However, Newton did not want to accept any hypothesis without experimental evidence. Action at a distance was after all a concept that science could well use to good advantage, and, for Newton, centres of force attracting at a distance were 'experimentally' and mathematically proved.

Some of the opponents of Newton felt that he should have given the world a mechanical explanation of motion through the assumption of ether. Mabilleau understood, as we have stated above, that Newton adopted the ether hypothesis. But, as has been pointed out above, when Newton was asked by Leibniz if he would not correspond with him concerning this matter Newton refused, but the challenge was taken up by one of Newton's defenders, Samuel Clarke. Again, Mabilleau says that Newton was forced to accept the ether hypothesis as a means to explain gravity in mechanical terms, because of the great force brought to bear upon him in 1710 by his school of disciples, especially by Clarke.[1] But, as has been pointed out and will also become more evident in the sequel, Clarke never accepted the ether hypothesis; much less would he urge Newton to accept it.

[1] *Histoire de la Philosophie Atomistique*, p. 442.

§ II

Newton's hypothetical analysis of the function of ether has given rise to the supposition that he had abandoned the emission theory of light, in which light is the function of the material particles emitted from luminous bodies, and that he had adopted a theory of light which resembles, if it is not identical in all its main features with, the undulatory theory. This opinion is due mostly to the misinterpretations of Thomas Young in his theory of light and colours.[1]

On 26 April 1694, Leibniz wrote to Huygens, stating, on the authority of Fatio d'Huillier, that Newton 'was more than ever led to believe that light consists of bodies which come actually to us from the sun'.[2] In the *Optics* of 1717 Newton restated his emission theory, asking : Is it not true that all the theories which suppose light to be a function of pressure or motion propagated through a fluid medium suppose light to arise also from new modifications of the rays ? Newton answered that this is erroneous.

If pressure propagated without actual motion is a result of light, Newton says, then light could not agitate and heat the bodies which refract and

[1] *Philosophical Transactions*, 1801 ; or *A Course of Lectures on Natural Philosophy and the Mechanical Arts*, 1845, vol. ii, p. 614 ; or Brewster, vol. i, pp. 146 ff.   [2] Brewster, vol. i, pp. 149–50.

reflect it. If, on the other hand, he pointed out, motion propagated to all distances in one moment of time is the result of light, ' it would require an infinite force every moment, in every shining particle, to generate that motion. And if it consisted in pressure or motion, propagated either in an instant or in time, it would bend into the shadow.' [1] But light, as a matter of fact—or so said Newton [2]—does not follow crooked passages nor bend into the shadow. Furthermore, this vibratory hypothesis could not explain refraction of light nor how rays could be alternately in ' fits of easy Reflection ' or ' easy Transmission ', unless they would suppose two types of ethereal vibrating mediums, and that is impossible, because through their mutual reaction upon one another they are bound to retard, shatter, disperse, and confound one another's motion. The function of ether, when Newton does admit such a medium, is to refract light rays, and it is the vibration of the particles that causes heat.

It seems to us erroneous and unwarranted to say that Newton at any time fully accepted the ether hypothesis as an instrument for the explanation of gravity or light. Not only did Newton, along

---

[1] *Optics*, 1717 ed., Qu. 28 ; see also Newton's objection to Hooke's theory of light.

[2] Einstein to the contrary.

with his school, strongly oppose any such interpretation, but, also, we have seen that Newton
invariably, after stating the possibility of the use
of a mechanical hypothesis, stated again and again,
with much certainty and vigour, his contrary,
if not contradictory, hypothesis of gravity. As
we have noted, Newton used the phrase ' for I
do not know what this ether is ', or ' for so I will
call it '.

But, on the other hand, it would be just as unjust
and dogmatic to say from the evidence at hand
that Newton thought it futile to explain gravity
by the aid of an ethereal medium. Some writers,
however, have held this. Lasswitz, for example,
says, after quoting from the preface of the second
edition of Newton's *Optics* : ' Geht schon hieraus
hervor, dass er die Ätherhypothese für sehr fraglich
hält, während ihm die Wirkung der Zentrifugal-
kräfte als den Erscheinungen entsprechend für
völlig gewiss gilt, so zeigt eine nähere Betrachtung
dessen, was er über die Natur dieses Äthers
beibringt, dass derselbe gar keine mechanische
Erklärung im Sinne einer kinetischen Theorie
liefert. Hätte Newton eine solche wirklich beab-
sichtigt, so hätte er ein Bewegungsgesetz angeben
müssen, nach welchem die Ätherteilchen bei
ihrer Berührung so aufeinander wirken, dass sie
die Erscheinungen der Gravitation an den Körpern

hervorbringen. Aber dies hat er nicht getan, nicht
einmal angedeutet. Die Gravitation sowie die
übrigen Energievermittelungen hat er allerdings
durch die Wirkung des Äthers ersetzt, aber nicht
durch eine mechanische Wirkung, sondern eben-
falls durch eine dynamische, durch eine nicht
weniger rätselhafte Eigenschaft als die Gravitation, nämlich, die Elastizität. Der Äther ist
elastisch, seine Elastizität aber beruht nicht wie
bei Huygens auf der durch ein mechanisches
Prinzip regulierten Agitation seiner Atome, sondern auf einer abstossenden Kraft derselben.' [1]

In answer to this it should be noted that men of
all ages have aimed to give a mechanical explanation of planetary motion. They noticed that the
heavenly bodies moved in geometrical relations, and
could readily see the likeness of their movements
to certain simple curves. Hippocrates, Apollon-
ius, Copernicus, and Kepler, each in his own way,
aimed to express these movements in terms of
geometrical properties. The same can be said of
Descartes, especially with reference to his *Principles*
and the *Meteors*, wherein he aimed to explain the
heavenly orbits as a geometrical order, even though
he never arrived at any single generalization or
geometrical formula. And although Democritus,

[1] Lasswitz, *Geschichte der Atomistik vom Mittlealter bis Newton*,
Hamburg, 1890, vol. ii, pp. 562–3.

Epicurus, and Lucretius did not concern themselves with final causes or explanations, they were interested in the explanation of phenomena, and aimed to give an explanation of secondary causes which, if it had not been for the general lack of mathematical symbolism, might have led to a celestial mechanics. However, it was really Huygens who gave the first clear mechanical idea of centripetal forces, which he supposed were the origin of all the central forces, stating that a body displaces itself in a uniform but circular movement. As early as 1673 he reduced these movements to the mathematical expression $F = \dfrac{V^2}{R}$.

Newton, despite Lasswitz, was no exception to the rule; he also tried to explain gravity in mechanical terms. He, being an atomist, followed the ancient atomists, and aimed to express the secondary causes of gravitational phenomena in mathematical terms, but he really went further, at least in his own mind; he was anxious to get at the 'real', or metaphysical, cause of gravity, and for this attempt he had two ways open to him: first, to explain gravity in mechanical terms by following the Cartesian, or accepting an ether hypothesis of his own; and, second, to follow Gilbert and Kepler by assuming that gravity is an attraction of the magnetic type (modern ideas of

electricity were not known).   Newton in 1695
wrote to Boyle that he believed in the ether
hypothesis of four years before, which could serve
as a mechanical explanation of light, of cohesion,
and also of repulsive forces.   Gravitation was,
in that scheme, bound up with molecular
mechanics, the centre of the universe being the
centre of absolute space and also the centre of
gravitation.[1]   As a matter of fact, this can be
shown to be true geometrically.

Newton also suggests a mechanical explanation
of gravity in the twenty-first query of the second
English edition of the *Optics*, as has been stated
above in another context.[2]

Of course, if Lasswitz would insist that a
' mechanical theory ' must be the modern kinetic

[1] *Optics*, 2nd ed., Qu. 24, and letter from Newton to Leibniz,
26 October 1693.

[2] For convenience' sake we may partly restate it here.   Let us
assume that a rare medium exists, which is composed of particles
which are elastic.   Again, let us assume that this ether is very
rare at the sun and gradually becomes more and more dense as it
is farther removed from the sun, increasing its density proportionally to the distance from the sun *ad infinitum* ; so that the
ether will be very dense near the planet Saturn, less dense near
the earth, and very rare near the sun.   Also, the elasticity of the
ether is proportional to the density and the ' vigour ' of the
ether increases proportionally with the density of it.   Therefore
any body would be naturally forced into the more rare parts of
the ether ; this power we call, says Newton, gravity.

theory, then we must say at once that Newton does not attempt to give one. Newton's theory, however, is just as much a ' mechanical one ' as the kinetic theory of to-day—the difference being that Newton's theory would be a rather static one, but nevertheless a ' mechanical one '.

The difficulty is that Newton's theory exists chiefly in the form of suggestions ; to understand his intention in full it will be profitable, therefore, to fill out his sketch as he himself might have done had he been faced by more modern problems. By hypothesis, as stated, a very fine ethereal medium exists ; this medium is elastic and very much resembles air or vapours. Now any substance which, like air, is highly compressible (and we assume that ether is such a substance, since it is by hypothesis, elastic), when inclosed in a closed system and revolved rapidly, will form different levels of density, being most rare at the very centre of the body and most dense at the outskirts of it.[1] If, therefore, any solid body which is not in motion should tend to the centre, it is necessary to conceive a mechanical arrangement of ether particles ; and Newton supposes such an arrangement. Furthermore, in any such system, as stated in footnote no. 2, p. 133, a body will actually tend from the dense regions towards

[1] *Optics*, 2nd ed., Qu. 28.

the rare ones, because the dense regions would exert more pressure upon any solid, while the rare regions would be less resistant, and naturally a body would move towards the least resistance, which would be, in Newton's system, towards the sun. But, it may be asked, is not the pressure of gases due to the violent movement of their particles, while Newton's ether, by hypothesis, is inert? That appears a serious objection at first glance, but we must remember that Newton always thought of ether as having density and ' vigour '; and by ' vigour ' he meant what we to-day call pressure, or resistance to compressive forces. It is true that this is an assumption, as great a one, in fact, as the assumption of centripetal force, but Newton was never conscious that this was a mere hypothesis. This was natural, for the thoughts of ether, by analogy, as some fine gas, and knowing that when gas is compressed, or in other words, becomes dense, it exerts a great pressure upon the closed system which contains it, he attributed ' vigour ' to ether.

The original ' God-given-motion ' of a planet is not only motion in a straight line, but also in a line of least resistance; so that the original motion plus the effect due to the pressure of ether particles, which effect is that of a force directed towards the sun, will result in the observed elliptic course of the planets, which is the same for mathematical purposes as the resultant of the original motion of a planet plus the pull of the sun upon it. Just as the ether is rare at the sun, so it is also to a very great degree rare near any large body, such as planets, satellites, or possibly the comets are ; therefore the same mechanical causes are in operation in terrestrial mechanics as in celestial.[1]

Our position may be reinforced by the following quotation from Newton's answer to Leibniz, 26 Oct. 1693—which, we may note, was written before his suggestions in the queries to the later editions of his *Optics* ; he says in part : ' . . . if any one should explain gravity and all its laws by the action of some subtle mediums, and should show that the motions of the planets and comets were not disturbed by this matter, I should by no means oppose it.'

The basis of fact in Lasswitz's contention is this : that Newton was very cautious in using as a scientific, and avoided using as a metaphysical, hypothesis, the existence of an ethereal medium in order to give a mechanical explanation of gravity ; and that may account for Newton's framing of his suggestion about ether in the form of questions at the end of his scientific work rather than as

[1] *Optics*, 2nd ed., Qu. 28.

assertions—a point to which we will come back at the end of the chapter.

What we are sure of at this point is : (1) that Newton definitely objected to the Cartesian explanation ; (2) that he did not want to commit himself fully to an ether hypothesis, both because of the lack of experimental evidence and the contradiction of some observed facts, and the very possible fear of theological complications ; and (3) that he was opposed to the Leibniz-Huygens idea of centripetal forces—not, however, because this idea was a basis of mathematical formulations, but because Leibniz and Huygens took the conception metaphysically.

§ III

There is other evidence in Newton's works which points to a different explanatory hypothesis of attraction, upon which Newton looked with more favour. This hypothesis was a metaphysical one. It was an attempt on the part of Newton to supply the primary cause, the underlying reason, the real explanation, of gravitational motion. Newton says, in the very last paragraph of the *Principia*—and this paragraph was never revised nor removed from any of the later editions of his work : ' Hitherto we have explained the phaenomena of the heavens and our sea by the power of Gravity, but have not yet assign'd the cause of this power. This is certain, that it must proceed from a cause that penetrates to the very centres of the Sun and Planets, without suffering the least diminution of its force; that operates, not according to the quantity of the solid matter which they contain, and propagates its virtue on all sides, to immense distances, decreasing always in the duplicate proportion of the distances. . . . And now we might add something concerning a certain most subtle Spirit, which pervades and lies hid in all gross bodies; by the force and action of which Spirit, the particles of bodies mutually attract one another at near distances, and cohere, if contiguous; and electric bodies operate to greater distances, as well repelling as attracting the neighbouring corpuscles; and light is emitted, reflected, refracted, inflected, and heats bodies; and all sensation is excited, and the members of animal bodies move at the command of the will, namely, by the vibrations of this Spirit, mutually propagated along the solid filaments of the nerves, from the outward organs of sense to the brain, and from the brain into the muscles. But these are things that cannot be explain'd in a few words, nor are we furnish'd with that sufficiency of experiments which is required to an accurate determination and demonstration of the laws by which

this electric and elastic Spirit operates.' And
with these puzzling statements Newton ends his
epoch-making book.

We cannot but be struck by the similarity of
description and function of this subtle electric
spirit and that of the ethereal medium quoted
above. At first glance a person is almost sure that
Newton is speaking about the same thing, but by
close examination clouds of mystery are thrown
about the subject. In order to disperse the clouds
and to throw some rays of light upon the mystery
of the above quotation we must examine in detail
certain documents written by Newton at the time
when he was completing those investigations the
result of which was the ideas stated in the
Principia.

The last few sentences of the *Principia* were
written about 1685, the whole work being completed the 8th of May 1686. On the 9th of
December 1675 Newton wrote a very detailed
account concerning his speculations about the
cause of attraction and change in general,[1]
and sent it, at the request of Oldenburg,[2] to the
Royal Society.

[1] ' A theory of light and colours, containing partly an Hypothesis to explain the properties of light discoursed of by him in
his former papers, partly the principal phenomena of the various
colours. . . .'

[2] Brewster, *op. cit.*, vol. i, pp. 133 ff.

Because of the bearing of this document upon our problem, and because of its general importance, we shall take the liberty of stating the main thesis of it in some detail : (1) Let us assume that there exists an ethereal medium, much the same as air, but far rarer, subtler, and more strongly elastic. But this medium is not homogeneous in substance ; on the contrary, it is composed partly ' of the main phlegmatic body of air intermixed with various vapours and exhalations. For the electric and magnetic effluvia and the gravitating principle seem to argue such variety.' At least ' electric effluvia ' warrant the assumption of the existence of such ethereal spirits. The attraction or movement of a piece of paper when it is within the close range of a piece of glass which has been rubbed can be explained only when we imagine the existence of such ethereal spirits. Because the substance contained within the glass, by ' rarefaction into an ethereal wind (for by its easy penetrating and circulating through glass, I esteem it ethereal) ', may cause the motions of the paper, and, by ' condensing ' again, may be the cause of electrical attraction of the paper towards the glass : ' so may the gravitating attraction of the earth be caused by the continual condensation of some other such like ethereal spirit ; *not of the main body of phlegmatic ether, but of*

*something very thinly and subtly diffused through
it, perhaps of an unctuous, or gummy tenacious, and
springy nature ; and, bearing much the same relations to ether which the vital aerial spirit requisite
for the conservation of flame and vital motions does
to air.*[1] For if such an ethereal spirit may be condensed in fermenting or burning bodies, or otherwise coagulated in the pores of the earth and water
into some kind of humid active matter for the
continual uses of nature (adhering to the sides of
those pores after the manner that vapours condense
on the sides of a vessel), the vast body of the earth,
which may be everywhere to the very centre *in
perpetual working,* may continually condense so
much of this spirit as to cause it from above to
descend with great celerity for a supply ; in which
descent, it may bear down with it the bodies it
pervades with force proportional to the superficies of all their parts it acts upon, nature making
a circulation by the slow ascent of such matter
out of the bowels of the earth in an aerial form,
which, for a time, constitutes the atmosphere, but,
being continually buoyed up by the new air,
exhalations, and vapours rising underneath, at
length . . . vanishes again into the ethereal spaces,
and there perhaps in time relents and attenuates
into its first principle. . . . *And, as the earth, so*

[1] Italics are ours.

*perhaps may the sun imbibe this spirit copiously,
to conserve his shining, and keep the planets from
receding further from him : and they that will may
also suppose that this spirit affords or carries with it
thither the solary fuel and material principle of light,
and that the vast ethereal spaces between us and the
stars are for a sufficient repository for this food of the
sun and planets. . . .'* In passing we may notice
the ring of Neo-Platonism found in the above
quotation from Newton ; we shall find similar
statements made by Gilbert and Boyle, &c., in the
following chapter.

(2) We may suppose that these ethereal spirits
are in a constant violent movement, and that they
may be the cause of reflection and refraction of
light and the cause of heat ; it may be supposed
that they are the chief means by which bodies are
fermented, purified, and melted. (3) These
spirits may also be the principal factors in the
cohesion of the parts of solids and fluids, ' of
the springiness of glass and other bodies '. (4)
And furthermore, this hypothesis may throw a
great deal of light upon the puzzling problem
' by what means the muscles are contracted and
dilated to cause animal motion '. For we may
suppose that there are ' animal spirits ', which are
neither like liquor, vapour, gas, nor spirits of wine ;
but of an ethereal nature which is contained

conveniently in the coats of the brain, nerves, and muscles.

(5) When we pour some oil into water the oil and water will not mix, while, on the contrary, if we pour some salt into water, they will mix perfectly. That may be explained through the existence of spirits, which ' by some secret principle of *unsociableness*, they keep asunder ; and some that are *sociable* may become *unsociable* by adding a third thing to one of them, as water to spirit of wine, by dissolving salt of tartar in it. The like unsociableness may be in ethereal natures, as perhaps between the ethers in the vortices of the sun and planets ; and the reason why air stands rarer in the pores of small glass pipes, and ether in the pores of bodies, may be, *not* want of subtilty, but sociableness ; and on this ground, if the ethereal *vital* spirit in a man be very *sociable* to the marrow and juices, and *unsociable* to the coats of the brain, nerves, and muscles, or to anything lodged in the pores of those coats it may be contained thereby.'

On the 28th of February 1679 Newton wrote a letter to Robert Boyle [1] in which he further develops his hypothesis of an ethereal spirit, and also suggests to Boyle the possibility of its use in chemistry, again assuring Boyle that this is

[1] Brewster, *op. cit.*, vol. i, pp. 409–19.

only a hypothesis and not a fact of empirical observation, and that he did not use it in any of his main works, because he was afraid of the controversy which this hypothesis might lead him into.

In this letter we find again a disposition towards a Neo-Platonic conception of the ether which is really more than a mere tendency. Newton says, among other things, the following : ' When any metal is put into common water, the water enters into its pores, to act on it and dissolve it. Not that water consists of too gross parts for this purpose, but because it is unsociable to metal. *For there is a certain secret principle in nature by which liquors are sociable to some things and unsociable to others. . . .*'

Newton closed this letter with a conjecture about the cause of gravity, which he claims just came upon him while writing this letter. The falling of bodies towards the earth may be due to the rarity of ether at the surface of the earth and the density of it as we move from the earth ; ether filling the pores of all bodies, a body far from the surface of the earth would contain dense ether within and around it, which naturally would give way to the more rare ether found as we approach the surface of the earth.

We can readily see that this tentative description of the cause of gravity is the same principle as the one used later by Newton, in his added question to the later editions of the *Optics*.

On the 20th of June 1686 Newton wrote to Halley, adding in the postscript to his letter the remark quoted above, and saying that, as the earth attracts bodies, so also the sun is kept shining and keeps the planets from getting away any farther from it by this *spirit*, which, we may say, also ' carries thither the solary fuel and material of light. . . .'—as ' the common cause of gravity towards the earth, sun and all the planets, and that, by this cause, the planets are kept in their orbits about the sun '.[1]

Newton, in his letters to Richard Bentley in 1692—these letters being general comments upon Bentley's lectures delivered upon Robert Boyle's foundation—says the following : ' The last clause of the second position I like very well. It is inconceivable that inanimate brute matter should, without the mediation of something else, which is not material, operate upon and affect other matter without mutual contact, as it must be, if gravitation, in the sense of Epicurus, be essential and inherent in it. And this is one reason why I

[1] Ball Rouse, W. W., *An Essay on Newton's Principia*, London, 1893, p. 161 ; this letter is found in full in the appendix of the book.

desired you would not ascribe innate gravity to me,[1] for I do not speak of gravity as essential and inherent to matter.'[2]

How can we fit in all of the above quotations with what has been previously discussed with regard to the ether hypothesis ? Has Newton in mind a new principle of attraction which is neither material not mechanically active, a metaphysical cause of gravity, or does he speak only in figurative terms ? Is Newton still speaking about the same material medium to which we have referred in the first parts of this chapter ? If not, and if there is a difference between the two hypotheses, what is the distinction ?

As we have already seen, Newton objected very vigorously against any material ' extension ', such as Descartes proposed, and also pleaded ignorance, in his main writings, as to the cause of gravity ; what he is sure of is that a universal rule —third law of motion—is manifested whenever attraction takes place. In his early and also in his later speculations about the cause of accelerated motion, Newton speaks of these new principles as an hypothesis that he is not at all certain about, because of lack of experimental evidence. Never-

---

[1] Bentley, *Sermons preached at Boyle's Lectures, &c.* Edited by Rev. A. Dyce, London, 1838, vol. iii, pp. 22 ff.

[2] *Op. cit.*, p. 210.

theless, in the closing paragraph of the *Principia*, the tone of assertion is not at all uncertain, but rather positive; he says, ' and now we may add something concerning a certain most subtile Spirit ', &c. His caution seems to have been due to the lack of experimental evidence; and he shunned controversy, which he hated, as he wrote to Oldenburg concerning these speculations: ' I had formerly purposed never to write any hypothesis of light and colours, fearing it might be a means to engage me in vain disputes; but I hope a declared resolution to answer nothing that looks like a controversy, unless possible at my own time upon some by-occasion, may defend me from that fear. . . .'[1] And that this hypothesis was not developed at a moment's notice, as he tells Boyle, is self-evidenced by its details and complexity: Newton must have thought a great deal about it.

Here, then, is the problem. On the one hand we have this most subtile spirit, this immaterial-vital-ethereal medium, which Newton referred to in his *Principia* and described in detail in his transactions with Oldenburg, Boyle, Halley, and Bentley—this metaphysical subtile spirit, which is everywhere and which is the cause of attraction, of magnetism, of electricity, of unity of organization between the particles of a body, of stability

---

[1] Brewster, *op. cit.*, vol. i, pp. 133–4.

or instability, and—since this spirit is at the command of the will—of animal motion ; which may be sociable or unsociable, which conserves the shining of the planets and keeps them from receding farther from the sun, which affords and carries with it the material principle of light, and which is stored in the vast repository of the interstellar ethereal spaces as food for the stars and the planets.   Thus in the thirty-first query of the *Optics*, Newton says, ' The *vis inertiae* is a passive Principle by which Bodies persist in their Motion or Rest, receive Motion in proportion to the Force impressing it, and resist as much as they are resisted.   By this Principle alone, there never could have been any Motion in the World.   Some other Principle was necessary for putting Bodies into Motion ; *and now they are in Motion, some other Principle is necessary for conserving the Motion*.   For from the various Compositions of two Motions, 'tis very certain that there is not always the same Quantity of Motion in the World. . . . Seeing therefore the variety of Motion which we find in the World is always decreasing, there is a necessity of conserving and recruiting it by active Principles, *such as are the cause of Gravity*, by which Planets and Comets keep their Motion in their Orbs, and Bodies acquire great Motion in falling ; and the cause of fermentation, by which the Heart and Blood of animals are kept in perpetual Motion and Heat; the inward Parts of the Earth are constantly warm'd, and in some places grow very hot ; Bodies burn and shine, mountains take Fire, the Caverns of the Earth are blown up, and the Sun continues violently hot and lucid, and warms all things by this light. . . . And if it were not for these Principles the Bodies of the Earth, Planets, Comets, Sun, and all things in them would grow cold and freeze, and become inactive masses ; and all Putrefaction, Generation, Vegetation, and Life would cease, and the Planets and Comets would not remain in their Orbs.' And again : ' It seems to me further, that these Particles have not only a *vis inertiae*, accompanied with such passive Laws of Motion as *naturally* result from that Force, but *also* that they are moved by *a certain active* Principle, such as is that of Gravity and . . .' [1] On the other hand, we have the *physical* hypothesis of the ether, which Newton set forth in the twenty-first question to the third edition of the *Optics*, as *not* the same kind of medium as the ' subtile spirit ', for here he gave a mechanical explanation of the ether, speaking of it in physical terms, describing it as a very subtile, rare medium of different degrees of density, which has vigour, which is the cause

[1] Italics are ours.

of attraction, of chemical action, and of animal motion, and which heats bodies and reflects light, &c. The question, then, is this: Did or did not Newton really conceive the ' subtile spirit '—an *immaterial* and *non-mechanical* entity—to be the same as the *mechanically* described ether?

§ IV

In order to answer more definitely the questions raised above, even though the final answer must always rest in the realm of probability, we must give a brief historical sketch of the ether hypothesis. This outline will necessitate some repetition of the ideas stated elsewhere.

The early Greeks thought of light, like fire, as being not material; they did not regard it as one of the elements. So later, Isaac Voss says that light is something real, and of the same type as sound, odour, vapour, and the magnetic force. Light is not a material substance, because it penetrates bodies. But after Grimaldi there was a tendency to return to a mechanical explanation of light, and in that regard ether was seriously discussed. Bonillan objected to Kepler's position, i. e. that the existence of ether is necessary to explain planetary motion. Bonillan thought that the planets within themselves have the necessary principle of motion, while Borelli even spoke in terms of action at a distance.

Hook and Boyle prepared indirectly the way to an abstract theory of ether. Like the Cartesian Rohault, Hook claimed that the cause of force and movement is to be found in the existence of extremely fine matter. Reflection and refraction of light is due, he thought, to unequal vibrations corresponding to different transparent bodies. Hook applied to astronomy, as to optics, the theory of elementary vibrations, and he aimed, in doing so, to reconcile the theories of Descartes and Grimaldi. Boyle's influence, however, was purely negative, pointing to the insufficiency of all the existing theories of light.

As has been noted before, the Cartesian mechanics was hostile to any hypothesis of ether as a medium by which motion is transferred ; it held that all motion is by impact or shock. Matter was never regarded by the Cartesians as the seat of forces, and to them it could never serve as a vehicle of forces, but only of movement. It was presupposed that the ethereal medium has the capacity to transfer not only movements, but the forces themselves. For this reason they were opposed to the assumption of a material, or immaterial medium ; in these respects they shared the opinions of the opposing school of Gassendi. Both also refused to believe, as Newton thought, that at the back of the atoms or of matter there exists something which is an objective centre of force, which propagates physical motion. This was also the reason why Huygens, who accepted central forces at first, finally came back to the impact or shock theory; the same was true of Bonillan; even Leibniz and Malebranche felt that Newton's suggestion of an ether hypothesis transcended the realm of mechanics and physics, in so far as it is taken to be an active medium of force transference with centres which propagate that force. It may be readily seen that even after Newton's explanation of it in the letter to Boyle the idea of an ether hypothesis was not regarded very highly in Newton's time, except possibly by Huygens. Scholars believed that the mechanical law of impact could explain all motion. While Newton would not oppose a mechanical theory, if it could be demonstrated to be true, he was almost certain that this could not be done for many reasons, experimental and theoretical, but primarily because of his theological conviction, which has been referred to. We may mention the following objection of Newton in the field of optics, i. e. his refusal to entertain the molecular theory of reflection. This theory would not permit the necessary continuity, which is all-important in optics as in physics generally. Why is it that the same substance will reflect light when polished

and will not do so before being polished ? The
light corpuscles are the same ; nevertheless they
are reflected in the first case and not in the second
case, in which they are partly diffused or absorbed
by the unpolished substance. Consequently it
is impossible to conclude that it is due to the
impact on the part of the corpuscles, and if this
is the cause of reflection, it must be due to a
reflective body acting as a whole upon a centre
which propagates light.[1] Newton felt that the
optical phenomena depend not only upon the
molecular properties of matter, but also upon the
spaces between the particles of matter.

In 1665–6 Newton was influenced by Borrow's
developing an interest in the problems of the day.
In 1669 Newton had no clear notion of the solu-
tion of the problems of optics. The year 1670
finds him with some notions about gravity, mainly
taken from some mystical stories, thinks Rosenberger.[2] In 1674 Newton's ideas on this matter
were vague and confused ; he was pre-occupied
with his mathematical and optical studies. In
this period Newton describes light in terms of
quasi-material movements ; the term ether was
never used. After 1671 and about 1675, that is,

[1] *Optics*, London, 1704, Book II, Princ. 3, Prop. 8.
[2] *Isaac Newton und seine Physikalishen Principien*, Leipsic,
1893, pp. 118–19.

during his dispute with Hooke, Newton is more and more cordial to the vibrating theory of light and to the ether hypothesis. From this time on Newton aimed to find a point of reconciliation of the emission and undulatory theories of light. This he hoped it would be possible to accomplish by some form of ether hypothesis. That hypothesis, however, was never regarded by Newton as being metaphysical, but rather as an auxiliary to science, which could not even be experimentally proved or verified. At that time he asked the following question in his communications : [1] Is light a material substance ? If it is, how do we know the fact ? Is the phenomenon of light a molecular property which Descartes denies ? Newton does not want to commit himself dogmatically ; probably Newton was not sure in his own mind at the time. He does not want to commit himself to the theory that light is material, nor to the opposite theory that it is an immaterial, incorporeal centre that produces light by emanation. He is certain that light is a body ; it possesses a reality *sui generis* ; but what kind of a body it is he would not decide. He would only pursue his experiments further.

At the end of 1675 Newton was partially converted to the undulatory theory of light. He

[1] Royal Society, 8 and 19 February, 1672.

thought that the ether hypothesis was as good as the emission hypothesis ; but nevertheless, even at this date, he would not commit himself altogether to the ether hypothesis, although he used it invariably. Newton thought that the rays of light do not consist in the movement of particles which are identical with material solids. He thought there must be in space a continued degradation of material resistance until one reaches centres which do not offer any resistance, which bear only a far likeness to corpuscular substances—and that is why ' the stars and the planets which move so freely and continuously without any sensible diminution in their movements, must be free of any corporeal fluid '. The centre in which the planets move must differ extremely from material centres, or, as Newton says in his *Optics* in regard to light, ' It is difficult to know if light is a projection of small corpuscles, or if it is only an abstract movement, a certain force which propagates itself.'

§ V

We are now able more assuredly to answer our original query : Does Newton posit in his later writings an hypothesis of ether—especially in order to explain light and gravitation—which is not at all a mechanical explanation ? Or does he

employ a material mechanical hypothesis of ether
to that end ?

As has been shown in the first section of
Chapter II, and in the above discussions in this
chapter, Newton never thought that the Cartesian
explanation of motion was a sound one. Nor did
he take very seriously the attempt to explain
gravity by a kinetic or physical means, assuming
the existence of an ethereal medium. The reasons
—if we may restate—were (1) that such a medium
would have produced resistance to planetary
motion, (2) that there were no reasons or experimental proof for the existence of such a medium,
and (3) that if we would reduce all forces to movements of matter as the primary causes of such
movements, we must assume the indestructibility
of such movements, that is, their continuity, if we
are to be assured that the universe itself is continuous. As we have noted, Descartes preserved
the continuity of movement by a metaphysical
hypothesis, while Leibniz replaced the quantity of
movement by the force of movement. Newton,
not seeing the importance of the continuity of
motion nor of force (conservation of energy) as
a necessary principle underlying the whole of
physics, especially because no conclusion followed
from the above principle, and, furthermore, no
experiment demanded it, concluded that it had no

physical foundations and that neither Descartes nor Leibniz needed to have recourse to a meta-physical explanation to maintain it. Newton pointed out that by the impact of even elastic bodies movement is always dispersed and some of it lost. The reason is that the bodies are not per-fectly elastic. He was sure that the transfer of motion from one body to another would necessarily destroy some part of the motion, due to friction ; e. g. in the case of liquids, bodies come to an equilibrium after a given time. Consequently, whenever any motion or change takes place some of its force or motion is lost, and, as a result of this, in time motion and change would cease. As things in the universe have been changing and moving for ever so long the motion and change would have stopped long ago if motion and change were not conserved by some principle. All of this points, says Newton, to the existence of an active principle or force, which compensates the loss, that is re-establishes the motion which is lost because of friction and impact. It was not until Newton's controversy with Hooke, about 1675, that he began to feel his way toward an hypothesis of some ethereal substance. But that was not, as Mabilleau points out, due to the criticism of Leibniz and Huygens and to the pressure of his disciples. The reason for Newton's suggestion that some type of ether hypothesis might be used was an attempt on his part to reconcile the emission and undulatory theories of light. But even then he thought of the ether concept as an hypothesis auxiliary to science rather than as an attempt to find a metaphysical explanation of light. But, once he began to consider such an hypothesis as a possible one, he considered it not as a simple physical hypothesis, but rather as an agent of all the transformations in the universe.[1] While Newton merely suggests such an hypothesis, nevertheless the suggestion lends itself to an expansion into a mechanical explanation of gravity. As he says : 'If any one should explain gravity and all its laws by the action of some subtle medium, and should show that the motion of the planets and comets was not disturbed by this matter, I should by no means oppose it.'[2] However, when Newton suggests an ether hypothesis, the ether is not of the type generally supposed in his day, but a much finer one, one that would offer hardly any resistance to celestial motion. But Newton, nevertheless, was not willing to answer the question he raised, which was : whether there is any identity between material bodies and the substance of ether. Further, whether bodies

---

[1] *Optics*, 3rd ed., Qu. 30.
[2] Newton's letter to Leibniz, 26 October 1693.

could not produce light by contact, and whether light, when condensed, could not become matter.[1]

Newton suggested an ether hypothesis only as a possible explanation of gravitation, but he is not at all sure that such an explanation is possible ; if such an explanation is developed without any experimental objections there is nothing to show that he would oppose it. What Newton is sure of, and what he insists upon, is his mathematical formulation of gravitational action as a law of nature. This law is not at all an attempt to give the causes of gravitation. Consequently Huygens's and Leibniz's objections to Newton's centripetal forces acting at a distance as represented in his mathematical law have no meaning. As Newton says, over and over again, ' I use the [attraction] here to signify only in general any force by which bodies tend towards one another, whatsoever be the cause. We must at first find out from experiment what are the bodies that do attract and repulse each other, and also the laws and properties of this mutual attraction and repulsion, before we may speak about the causes of this attraction and repulsion.'[2] And again he says, 'These principles are not occult qualities, but rather general laws of nature by which things are formed.'[3]

[1] Last question of the third edition of his *Optics*.
[2] *Optics*, 3rd ed., Qu. 30.   [3] *Ibid.*, Qu. 31.

This law of gravitation is mathematical; it is an algebraic expression of the ways bodies act or move; and, also, it is empirical; that is, it can be experimentally verified, and, therefore, it is of primary importance to mechanics. It is an attempt to replace old notions of affinity or impulsion by concepts of attraction mathematically expressed and experimentally verified. Mathematical laws which would make our calculation of scientific value, and do not give us the causes of forces, are very important to physics. Whether these causes of gravitational motion are the same or not is not a problem of physics; in physics we give the same mathematical or empirical expressions, or the same name to the same effects, even if the causes are not the same. Newton knew that it is the effects that we express and deal with. It is because the effects of terrestrial gravity are the same as the effects of celestial gravity that we give them both the same mathematical expression, and this, of course, leads to the idea of universal gravitational laws or universal attraction, or any other word that we might use to represent these universal effects. The mathematical formula will always be the same, or, to put it in other words, the ratio of relationship between the different factors within the formula will always be the same, whether expressed in Euclidean or any other type

of geometrical system. In fact, we may represent
the constancy of this law as actually taking place
in terms of emanation, or as produced by the
action of ether, or of air, &c., whether it is material
or spiritual. In every case the effects or motion
of the phenomena, if followed in the same
relationship, would be expressed by the same
mathematical formula, because this formula is a
result of the observations of this effect or motion.
Here lies the greatness of a mathematical description.

The law of gravitation describes a fact; as
Newton thought, it is deduced from the appearance of movement; it is not, however, an
expression of the cause of movement. Newton
points out also in his letter to Bentley that he
cannot see how men educated in philosophy
could ever assume seriously that gravitation
should be an attribute of matter, so that one body
could attract another at a distance through empty
space; there must be an agent, an intermediary
which would transfer action or force from one
body to another, but, on the question whether
this is material or immaterial, he would not want
to commit himself. As a mathematical physicist
Newton did not have to answer that question. In
fact, he laid down a rule in physics against any
unnecessary or metaphysical hypothesis. Whether

he follows that rule completely will be discussed later. Universal gravity is a scientific fact ; it is the first truly positive scientific theory, and not an attempt at a metaphysical theory like the theory of Descartes, Leibniz, or Tycho-Brahe.

Newton, however, goes beyond the needs of mathematical physics, referring to and constantly suggesting the metaphysical cause of gravity. In his most significant objection to the Cartesian explanation, discussed above with reference to the attempt to preserve the constancy of motion or force, he points to the necessary existence of some active principle of force which would conserve and compensate lost motion. Newton did not take very seriously the attempt to explain this conservation mechanically, as has been noted above from his letters to Bentley, saying that gravitation must be caused by an agent following certain laws. He is willing to have Cotes [1] refer to the fact that it is the Creator who by his will produces gravitational action. The same references are to be found in the words written by Newton himself [2] and in the writings of Newton's best defenders ; [3] also Samuel Hosley, the editor

---

[1] Newton, *Principia*, 2nd ed., Preface.

[2] As pointed out above, especially at the end of the third book of the *Principia*, and in the questions to the *Optics*.

[3] Clarke, Samuel ; also Rohault's *Natural Philosophy and*

of Newton's *Opera*, says that the originator and
sustainer of gravity is not material but divine, and
that Newton did not explain his laws in terms of
repulsion but in terms of immaterial causes, not
perceivable to the senses, but manifested to the
spirit and effected by God.[1] Now it becomes
clear why Newton so rigorously tried to show that
motion, force, attraction, or gravitation is not
a property or attribute of matter. While inertia,
mobility, penetrability, hardness, and size are
qualities of matter, as was pointed out in Chapter
II, attraction is not. Attraction is more extensive,
it is a universal quality of the cosmos. Universal
gravity would be impossible without the assumption of an active principle outside of matter
acting upon it. The attribute of inertia is purely
passive, and that is the reason that we must
assume an active principle that not only moves
matter, but also, which would conserve motion,
making it constant, because of the loss due to
friction. Newton felt that if we would assume
that attraction is an attribute of matter there
would be no need for a Creator, and he hoped that

Physics, p. 573. See Rohault's *Tractatus Physicus*, London,
1682. This book is of interest as it is the first school text
of Newton's physics which was introduced into the schools in
place of Descartes's physics because it did not contradict the
existence of God.

[1] *Opera*, Tom. I, Dedicatio ad Regem, p. 3.

his *Principia* would be a proof of the existence of a God, conceived in theistic terms.[1] These active principles which are the cause of attraction Newton called centripetal forces in his mathematical physics.

In his metaphysical moments Newton speaks of the active principle in terms of *spiritus* as quoted fully above. *Spiritus* is not a mechanical or mathematical expression; it is a metaphysical one. As he says, to quote again : 'Hitherto we have explained the phenomena of the heavens and of our sea by the power of gravity, but have not yet assigned the cause of this power. This is certain, that it must proceed from a cause that penetrates to the very centres of the sun and planets without suffering the least diminution of its forces. . . . And now we might add something concerning a certain most subtle spirit which pervades and lies hid in all gross bodies ; by the force and action of which spirit . . . bodies attract, . . . cohere, . . . light is limited. . . .' Again : ''Tis very certain that there is not always the same quantity of motion in the world. . . . Seeing, therefore, the variety of motion which we find in the world is always decreasing, there is a necessity of conserving and recruiting it by active Principle, such as are

---

[1] Letters to Bentley ; also *Mémoires de l'Académie Royale*, Paris, 1732, p. 347.

the cause of gravity. . . .' And again : ' Particles
have not only a *vis inertiae*, accompanied with such
passive laws of motion, but also that they are
moved by a certain active principle, such as is
that of gravity. . . .' (*Optics*, 3rd ed., Qu. 31.)
From these utterances we notice that gravity is
distinct from matter and from mechanical forces.
Gravitation is caused by an agent which acts constantly according to well-defined laws. Newton
concluded from the fact of centripetal forces
acting at a distance the existence of an *immaterial*
principle which is the cause of gravity. As Lasswitz
points out, it is from the law of gravitation and from
observed facts that Newton comes to the conclusion that it is not matter which has the faculty of
motion, but that motion is caused by an immaterial
principle.[1]

§ VI

To summarize, we may say that Newton conceived his mathematical expression of gravity not
as a real explanation of the causes of gravity but
rather as an empirical law, as an algebraically

[1] *Geschichte der Atomistik von Mittelalter bis Newton*, Hamburg, 1890, vol. i, p. 578. Lasswitz also calls the reader's
attention to the fact that Zöllner, because of his mystical sense,
was guided rightly in his understanding of Newton. The title
of the latter's work is *Prinzip. d. elektrodyn. Theorie, &c.* . . .
Leipzig, 1876. See also Isenkrahe, C., *Das Räthsel von der
Schwerkraft*, 1879, pp. 11 ff., 15.

expressed and experimentally verified fact of nature. Newton knew that the science of physics did not demand any further explanation ; nevertheless, he does suggest directly in the questions to his *Optics* and in a letter to Boyle a possible mechanical explanation of the cause of gravitation, by the assumption of a new ether hypothesis. Some such mechanical explanation Newton thinks it might be possible to develop, and, if free from all empirical objections, he would not oppose it. On the other hand, Newton suggests indirectly and directly throughout his whole works another possible explanation which would contain the causes of gravity — an explanation the very opposite to a mechanical one ; it is a metaphysical hypothesis of the existence of immaterial principles, which not only move matter directly, but also conserve its motion, or re-create the motion which is lost because of friction. It is because of this metaphysical assumption that we can understand Newton's refusal to believe in material forces acting at a distance, even though such an action is mathematically proved ; it is because it is not material force but immaterial force which moves and acts upon matter without any *material* medium between them, the medium being also immaterial, i. e. space. It is God as an agent acting through a medium of space upon matter, space being the 'Sensorium of God'. But about these metaphysical causes we have no mathematical or experimental proof. This explanation, if accepted at all by Newton, was accepted only dogmatically, as that of the existence of God, because he felt that proof of metaphysical causes is only possible as a result of, or comes at the end of, complete scientific knowledge. And because of this Newton was extremely cautious. While he was willing to approve the unqualified statements of his followers on this point, he himself would rather not commit himself, even if his own convictions were strong. His scientific temper and his own character would not allow him to become fully responsible for theories which he could not prove. His whole theological thinking, his studies in Jacob Boehme, William Yworth, and others of that type, his own associates and followers, all of them cried for proof of, for an expression of, a theological, theistic world ; they demanded once for all the overthrow of all physics which would make atheism possible and a development of natural philosophy which would be the indisputable proof of God's existence. That would explain Newton's letter to Bentley in which he says : 'When I wrote my treatise [the *Principia*] about our system, I had an eye upon such principles as might work with considering men for the belief of a Deity ; and nothing can rejoice me more than to find it useful for that purpose.' That hope was found in Newton's suggestion of inert matter moved freely by immaterial principles by the agency of its Creator and through the medium of space, the sensorium of God, according to a purpose willed by God which could be expressed mathematically in terms of a formula.

We will discuss in the next chapter the nature of this metaphysical hypothesis as understood by Newton and also by his forerunners and contemporaries.

IV

NEWTON'S METAPHYSICAL DOCTRINE OF GRAVITY

§ I

In this chapter we shall discuss the metaphysical aspects of Newton's conception of a possible cause of gravity. Newton suggested that we need to assume the existence of some active principles which are the cause of motion ; he called these, most of the time, 'Ethereal Spirits', or simply 'Spirits'. If we want to investigate the origin or the real cause of motion we must plunge into the realm of metaphysics. Before we discuss Newton's meaning of 'active principles' or 'ethereal spirits' and point out the probable sources of influence, it will be well to point out briefly how that expression was generally used. In the days of Empedocles and Hippocrates (5–4 century B.C.) men wrote of something derived from the outer air being present for the use of the organism, in the vessels which also contain the blood.[1] They called it 'pneuma' or 'air in

---

[1] Aristotle, 'On Restoration', in *Aristotelis Opera*, Edidit Academia Regia Borussica, Berlin, 1831–70, 473*a*, 15 to 474*a*,

motion ', or what we mean by the word gas, vapour, steam, exhalation, emanation. The Latin word equivalent to ' pneuma ' is ' spiritus ', the English derivative being ' spirits '. While Aristotle used ' pneuma ' as either innate or what appears to be a vapour produced within the body itself by heat or by disease, the physicians of his time revived and handed down the idea that not only blood but a derivative of the air is distributed through the body by means of vessels. More than four hundred and fifty years later Galen modified this important doctrine of a Greek physician Erasistratus (about 300 B.C.), who believed that there are special vessels for the blood and for spirits derived from the air. Galen incorporated the vital spirits in the arteries with the blood.[1] ' Animal spirits ' was one of the technical terms of physiology. The term *animal* does not refer to lower creatures as opposed to man, but is used in its obsolete original sense of ' pertaining to the soul ', for which latter the Latin word was *anima*, the Greek word *psyche*. We might best translate the original Greek expression *pneuma psychikon*,

24; also, Hippocrates, 'On the Sacred Disease', in *Œuvres Complètes d'Hippocrate*, traduction nouvelle, par E. Littré, Paris, 1839–61, vol. vi, pp. 368, 372.

[1] ' Is blood naturally contained in the arteries ? ' in *Claudii Galeni Opera Omnia*, ed. C. G. Kuhn, Leipzig, 1821–33, vol. iv, pp. 703, 736.

or the Latin *spiritus animalis*, into the English of to-day *psychical spirits*. However, the notion of ' animal spirits ' was of the highest physiological importance. Galen took it as ' the first instrument of the soul ',[1] and it assumed the same high position as Aristotle's native heat. For Galen, the animal spirits were the medium of sensation and volition, and were imported by the ventricles of the brain to the special cord and nerves, the fibres of which were believed, accordingly, to consist of tubes in which the ' subtlest animal spirits ' were contained, the bore of these tubes being too small to be visible.[2]

Although Harvey emphatically argued against Scaliger and Fernelius, who held that in the blood exist aerial, ethereal, or both ethereal and elemental spirits, constituting ' animate heat more excellent and more divine ', and claimed that the ' innate heat ' is the result of ' the living blood ',[3] nevertheless Harvey, like Aristotle before him, thought that the ' heat in animals which is not fire and does not take its origin from fire ' derives its origin from the ' solar ray '. As Harvey said :

[1] Galen on the Doctrine of Hippocrates and Plato, *op. cit.*, vol. v, p. 608.

[2] Curtis, *Harvey's Views on the Use and Circulation of the Blood*, Columbia University Press, 1915, pp. 20, 22, 23.

[3] ' On Generation ', in *The Works of William Harvey*, trans. by R. Willis, London, 1847, lxxi, 504, i. 16.

' The blood, when present within the veins as part of a body, a generative part, too, and endowed with soul, being the soul's immediate instrument, and primary seat . . . the blood, seeming also to have a share of another diviner body and being suffused with divine heat, suddenly acquires extraordinary powers, and is analogous to the elements of the stars. As spirits, the blood is the hearth, the vesta, the household deity, the innate heat, the sun of the microcosm, the fire of Plato ; not because it shines, burns, and destroys like common fire, but because it preserves, and nourishes, and increases its very self by its per-petual wandering motion . . . constructs and adjoins to itself, even as the heavenly bodies above, especially the sun and moon, impart life to what is below, while they continue in perpetual circula-tion. Since, therefore, the blood acts beyond the powers of the elements, and is potent with those virtues aforesaid, and also is the instrument of the supreme workman, no one ever will give praise enough to its wonderful and divine faculties.' [1] Here we may find an attempt at a metaphysical and divine explanation of the nature of the blood. We may find similar notions in Newton, when he speaks of physiological ether, which is the cause

[1] 'On Generation,' in *The Works of William Harvey*, trans. by R. Willis, London, 1847, lxxi, 510, i. 15–40.

of ' animal motion which heats bodies. . . .',
as pointed out in the preceding chapter.

The idea of ' Ethereal Spirits ' or ' Spirits ' was
generally used as a metaphysical principle because
of an attempt to explain the nature of Being.
It was especially used by the Neo-Platonists and
the Mystics generally. As has been just explained,
the special use of the same concept—*animal
spirits*, *pneuma*, *spiritus*, especially psychical spirits
or physiological ether—was quite common among
the physicians before Newton's time, in one way
or another. Its general usage can be found
throughout certain types of metaphysical speculations ; e. g. the immaterial world becomes the
world of mind and spirit, for it was thus changed
that the world of Platonic ' ideas ' passes to future
generations, at the hands of Plotinus, the Neo-
Platonist ; the bodiless, but yet not mental or
spiritual, archetypes ' of the world of experience
are taken up into the inward nature of mind '.
The doctrine of the *pneuma* is united with
Aristotle's God, ' by conceiving of the forces of
nature's life as the working of pure Spirit '. [1]

In the attempt to explain gravity we find
William Gilbert using the doctrine of ethereal
spirits as early as the beginning of the seventeenth

[1] Windelband, *History of Philosophy*, trans. by Tufts, pp.
233, 236.

century.[1] Whether Newton knew of Gilbert's
investigations at first hand is very hard to determine. Brewster never mentions even the name
of Gilbert, but, as we well know, Brewster very
seldom speaks about the relations of Newton
with older scientists, and when he does he speaks
only about the greatest or most immediate forerunners of Newton—Euclid, Kepler, Descartes—
although Newton, who began to study only about
fifty years after the appearance of Gilbert's books,
must almost certainly have read the works of this
physicist, for the latter was regarded throughout
learned Europe as the 'father of the magnetic
philosophy'[2] and the 'father of experimental
philosophy',[3] and his book created a powerful
impression at the time. Galileo expressed the
highest admiration for it ; it was indeed by the
'perusal of *De Magnete* that Galileo was induced
to turn his mind to magnetism'.[4] Priestley

[1] Gilbert is probably the most thorough-going and the ablest
prophet of the inductive method.

[2] Translator's Preface, p. 5, to William Gilbert of Colchester,
Physician of London, on the *Loadstone and Magnetic Bodies, and
on the Great Magnet, the Earth ; a new Physiology, Demonstrated
with many arguments and experiments* ; translated by P. Fleury
Mottelay, New York, 1893.

[3] *Op. cit.*, Preface, p. 13 ; and also called by Poggendorff ' the
Galileo of Magnetism ' (*Geschichte der Physik*, p. 286).

[4] Munk, *Roll of the Royal College of Physicians*, 1878, p. 78.

called him ' the father of modern electricity '.[1]
If Newton had not actually read Gilbert's works,
he must have been familiar with Gilbert's results
through his intimate connexion with Boyle, who
spoke of Gilbert and his investigations in many
different connexions, of which we may quote the
following one : ' It may now, therefore, be not un-
seasonable to confess to you that I have some
faint suspicions that besides those more numerous
and uniform sort of minute particles that are by
some of the new philosophers thought to compose
the ether, I lately discoursed of, there may possibly
be some other kind of corpuscles fitted to have
considerable operations, when they find con-
gruous bodies to be wrought on by them. . . . This
suspicion of mine will seem the less improbable if
you consider, that, though in the ether of the
ancients there was nothing taken notice of but
a diffused and very subtle substance, yet we are at
present content to allow that there is always in the
air a swarm of steams moving in a determinate
course betwixt the north pole and the south ;
which substance we should not *probably have
dreamed of*, if our inquisitive Gilbert had not
happily found out the magnetism of the terrestrial
globe. And few, perhaps, would have imagined,
that when a hunted and wounded deer has hastily

---

[1] Mottelay's Preface, p. 73, to trans. of *De Magnete*.

passed over a little grass, he should leave upon it such determinate, though invisible *effluvia,* as should for many hours impregnate the air, as to betray the individual flying and unseen deer.' [1]

Gilbert thinks of magnetic attraction as coming not from any mathematical point in the centre of a loadstone, but rather from all and every part of the whole magnet—as members of that whole—the attraction of the parts nearer the poles being stronger.[2]

A magnetic body also may magnetize a number of non-magnetic bodies without losing any of its attractive powers, because of the awakening of potential magnetic tendencies in so-called non-magnetic bodies.[3] Therefore we may say that all bodies are magnetic bodies whether their magnetic attraction be potential or actual. Newton, like Gilbert, thought also, as we have seen, that the ' force ' of a body is the sum total of forces of each particle of which the body is composed. We must always keep in mind that Newton put in the same category all attracting forces, whether their function be gravity, magnetism, or electricity.

Gilbert claimed that the earth is a great load-

---

[1] Boyle, *Cosmical Suspicions, Appendix to the Cosmical qualities of Things,* vol. iii, pp. 316–17.

[2] Gilbert, *Loadstone and Magnetic Bodies, &c.,* pp. 23–4, 313.

[3] Cf. *ibid.,* p. 61.

stone; it exhibits the same characteristics of attraction as any small or great loadstone does.[1] The interior of the earth, he thought, is composed of a homogeneous magnetic mass;[2] the movements of the earth 'are impulsions of homogeneous parts towards one another or towards the primary conformation of the whole earth'.[3] It is also due to magnetic attraction, he held, that the small parts of the earth are held together; for instance, parts of iron are held together by a magnet.[4] It may be wondered how such a great mass as the earth can be held together by magnetic force, but this wonder is dispersed when we know that the force is always proportional to the quantity or mass of a body; and we know, experimentally, that the greater the mass of a loadstone the greater is its force of attraction.[5] As the force of the earth is a result of the forces of its parts, so also, said Gilbert, the movement of the earth is a result of the movement of its parts; because the parts of the earth move in circles the whole earth must move in a circle.[6]

From the above, as well as from some points to be stated later, Gilbert developed two general axioms or rules: (1) that 'the matter of the

---

[1] Cf. *ibid.*, p. 64.
[2] Cf. *ibid.*, p. 69.
[3] Cf. *ibid.*, p. 72.
[4] Cf. *ibid.*, p. 142.
[5] Cf. *ibid.*, pp. 152, 155.
[6] Cf. *ibid.*, p. 331.

earth's globe is brought together and held together by itself electrically ; (2) that the earth's globe is directed and revolves magnetically '.[1] In these two rules we may find the first expression of terrestrial electricity and magnetism.[2]

There is another phenomenon of attraction— the attraction exhibited by sapphire, carbuncle, iris stone, opal, amethyst, vincentina, English gem, beryl, rock crystal, amber, jet, and diamond, when rubbed, which phenomenon of attraction we may call ' electric force '.[3] To the above list of ' electrics ' developed by Gilbert, Boyle added another one called ' resinous cake '.[4] All ' electrics ' attract objects of every kind, but they never ' repel or propel ' any.[5]

How this attraction, magnetical or electrical, takes place, was discussed by Gilbert at length under the heading ' Magnetic Coition '.[6] Experimentally, Gilbert had determined that many different ' electrics ' exhibit the same type of attraction ; therefore it follows, he thought,

---

[1] Gilbert, *Loadstone and Magnetic Bodies, &c.*, p. 97.

[2] Humboldt, *Cosmos*, 1849, vol. ii, p. 727.

[3] Gilbert, *op. cit.*, p. 77.

[4] *Encyc. Brit.*, article ' Electricity '.

[5] Gilbert, *op. cit.*, p. 176.

[6] Cf. *ibid.*, Book II, chap. ii, pp. 74–97. This chapter exhibits also a very fine example of very early but good employment of experimental method.

that the attractive force of any one of the 'electrics' is not due to the peculiar property of that 'electric'; e.g. the attractive force of amber is not due to the individually peculiar properties of amber.[1] Then, what is it, asked Gilbert, that produces or is responsible for the attractive forces characteristic of bodies? What is it that produces movement? Is it the body itself 'circumscribed by its contour'?[2] Or is it something insensible flowing out of a 'magnetic or electric' body into the air? And if it is an imperceptible 'flowing out of' or 'effluvium', does it set the air in circular motion, and are the bodies within that whirlwind set into motion by it? Or are the bodies directly driven up by this effluvium? But if the body attracts another by itself, what is the need of friction caused by rubbing, providing the surface of the body is 'clean and free from adhesions'?[3] That the body is neither set in motion by itself nor by

[1] Cf. *ibid.*, p. 81.

[2] This concept of effluvium later was greatly developed by Boyle in the following works: (1) *Of the Strange Subtility of Effluviums*, 1673, pp. 38–42, 52, 53; (2) *Of the Great Efficacy of Effluviums*, 1673, pp. 18, 19, 32, 33; (3) *Of the Determinate Nature of Effluviums*, 1673, pp. 21, 57; (4) *An Essay about . . . Gems*, 1672, pp. 108–12. (The above references are to *The Works of the Honourable Robert Boyle*, first ed., London.)

[3] Gilbert, *op. cit.*, p. 87.

the air is demonstrated experimentally ;[1] hence, it is very probable that a magnetic or electric such as we find in amber ' exhales something peculiar that attracts the bodies themselves, and not the air. . . .[2] A breath, then, proceeding from a body that is a concretion of moisture or aqueous fluid, reaches the body that is to be attracted, and as soon as it is reached it is united to the attracting electric ; and a body in touch with another body by the peculiar radiation of effluvia makes of the two one : united, the two come into most intimate harmony, and that is what is meant by attraction.'[3] So attraction takes place, according to Gilbert, by means of immediate contact[4] due to the effluvium, and not by action at a distance.

To show at this point the close similarity of ideas between Newton and Gilbert we need only recall the function of ethereal spirits—or what Newton also calls effluvia—when applied to magnetic or electrical forces as the principle which directly, by means of contact, draws together or asunder particles of matter.

All electrical attraction, Gilbert thought, is effected by means of moisture ;[5] and this attraction takes place in reference to all bodies,

---

[1] Gilbert, *op. cit.*, pp. 87–90. [2] Cf. *ibid.*, p. 89.
[3] Cf. *ibid.*, p. 91. [4] Cf. *ibid.*, p. 92.
[5] Cf. *ibid.*, pp. 92, 93, 94.

save flame and 'thinnest air'.[1] The 'peculiar efluvia of electrics, being the subtilest matter of solute moisture, attract corpuscles'. The earth's effluvium unites parts of matter that are separated, and the earth, by its means, brings bodies to itself from the atmosphere; otherwise, why should bodies 'seek the earth from the heights'?[2] How this effluvium operates so that bodies would be attracted by it is explained by Gilbert in the following way: 'Thinner effluvia lay hold of the bodies with which they unite, enfold them, as it were, in the arms, and bring them into union with the electrics; and the bodies are led to the electric source, the effluvia having greater force the nearer they are to that.'[3] In this explanation of the operation of an effluvium we have the opportunity to see the 'mystic' concept of attraction worked out to its logical conclusions, while later writers, using the same concept, conscious of its mystic rather than empirical basis, 'explain' the operation of effluvia or 'non-material, ethereal spirits' in terms of analogy or metaphors, like Gassendi, or plead ignorance when asked about details, like Newton.

The same clearness of ideas was manifested by Gilbert when he dealt with the question whether

[1] Cf. *ibid.*, pp. 95, 96.   [2] Cf. *ibid.*, p. 92.
[3] Cf. *ibid.*, p. 95.

effluvia emitted are corporeal or incorporeal. Gilbert asked, is that which ' subsists emitted ' nothing ? If the effluvium be considered as a body it must be *light* and *spiritual* in order that it may enter dense bodies, as experience shows it does, answered Gilbert. Hence, that which emanates is non-corporeal or non-material.[1] When Gilbert spoke of attractive forces or effluvia as being spiritual, non-corporeal, he does not mean what we to-day generally mean by spiritual, something divine, or like ' soul-substance ', *but rather something extremely thin, e.g. a breath, very thin air, or vapour. It is not material, because some of its qualities or characteristics are different from those of matter. Matter is hard, impenetrable, inert, movable, and extended, whereas a non-corporeal effluvium is penetrable, it is the principle of motion and attraction—it moves inert matter—though it, too, is extended. This distinction is of the same nature as Aristotle's distinction between form and matter, form being immaterial. What is true of Gilbert, in this respect, we shall see later, is true of Boyle, Newton, More, Clarke, and the Cambridge philosophers of that day.*

If we should now ask what is responsible for the position and movement of our earth ? what is the cause of the order and regularity of all the motions

[1] Gilbert, *op. cit.*, pp. 106, 109.

and revolutions of the planets ? and is this apparent order fixed and determined or 'pathless' ? —Gilbert would answer these queries by imagining the existence of a 'soul' which is different in different globes. Each homogeneous part tends to its own globe and follows the direction common to the whole world, the forms or souls of the different globes being effused and projected in a sphere all round it, and having their own bounds, making it necessary for the different planets to have their well-defined orbits, and the general order of the cosmos being the result of it.[1] This soul—in the interior of the globe—is confined as in a prison cell ; it can send its ' effused immaterial forms ' only within the limits of its own sphere, and bodies are put in motion by it only by ' great labour and exertion '.[2]

Like the earth, so also all the heavenly bodies, being set down, as it were, in their destined orbits, contain all the elements or parts which bear a relation to their particular centres, the parts being assembled around them, Gilbert said. If these parts have motion, their motion will be one of rotation about these centres, as in the rotation of the earth, or they will move in an orbit like that of the moon.[3] All the heavenly

[1] Cf. *ibid.*, p. 308.   [2] Cf. *ibid.*, p. 311.
[3] Cf. *ibid.*, p. 320.

bodies have circular motion, and, because this
motion is a natural motion, they revolve ' un-
troubled by any ill or peril ' ; they move ' under
no external compulsion ' ; there is nought to
make resistance, nothing to give way before it, but
the path is open. For, since they revolve in a
space void of bodies, the *incorporeal* ether, all
atmosphere, all emanations of land and water, all
clouds and suspended meteors rotate with the
globe : the space above the earth's exhalations is
a vacuum ; in passing through a vacuum even the
lightest bodies and those of least coherence are
neither hindered nor broken up.[1]

As we have noted, Gilbert spoke of ether as
being incorporeal ; that concept of ethereal substance, which had its beginning in early Greek
philosophy, runs also through the writings of the
Cambridge philosophers before and in Newton's
time.

Gilbert developed the concept of the universality
of natural causes : the earth merely shows the
phenomena demonstrated on a much larger scale
by the whole creation ; the earth is a mere
' mite and amid the mighty host of many thou-
sands, [it] is lowly, of small account, and de-
formate '. ' And for us ', said Gilbert, ' we deem
the whole world animate, and all globes, all

[1] Gilbert, *op. cit.* p. 326.

stars, and this glorious earth too, we hold to be from the beginning by their own destinate souls governed and from them also to have the impulse of self-preservation.' [1] Whatever is in nature moves naturally : all bodies are impelled by their own forces and by a consentient compact of other bodies. Such is universally true of all behaviour, whether it be the minute part of any whole, or any great globe and star.[2] The sun, thought Gilbert, is the chief ' inciter ' to action in nature ; the ' sun is the cause of the rotation of the planets, and also the cause of their revolution by sending forth energies from the sun's sphere, the sun's light being effused from it '.[3]

Whether Newton received any definite hint from Gilbert that the laws of the planets apply to the whole cosmos, or that the universe is fundamentally a simple order of relations, cannot be definitely proved. What we may say is that Gilbert developed this idea to a certain extent, but, on the other hand, he never developed in detail a definite notion of mechanical action. The similarity between Gilbert and Newton is again apparent in the function of the sun and the origin and nature of light. Gilbert also hinted, very definitely, at the relation of the earth to the

[1] Cf. *ibid.*, p. 309. [2] Cf. *ibid.*, p. 322.
[3] Cf. *ibid.*, pp. 333–4.

moon, saying, in his posthumous work *De Mundo nostro Sublunari Philosophia nova* (1631): ' The force which emanates from the moon reaches to the earth, and, in like manner, the magnetic virtue of the earth pervades the region of the moon: both correspond and conspire by the joint action of both, according to a proportion and conformity of motions, but the earth has more effect in consequence of its superior mass ; the earth attracts and repels the moon, and the moon, within certain limits, the earth ; not so as to make the bodies come together, as magnetic bodies do, but so that they may go on in a continuous course.' [1] Here again, as before, it cannot be ascertained whether Newton knew about this doctrine of Gilbert's. However, whether or not Newton owed a debt to Gilbert, his real predecessors after all were the greater names of Copernicus, Galileo, and Kepler.

As has been stated above, Boyle referred to Gilbert as the great forerunner of the concept of effluvia in the field of magnetic and electrical action. Boyle extended this concept, using it generally as a means of explaining all types of attraction and repulsion. It is the effluvium or ethereal spirits which are the causes of the stability or instability of bodies in chemical action;

---

[1] See also, Whewell, W., *History of Inductive Sciences,* 1859, vol. i, p. 394.

it is due to them that corpuscles stick together to form any body ; and so forth. In Boyle's use of this concept the similarity between his use of it and that of Newton is much more apparent, in its details, than between the usages of Newton and Gilbert. However, we find the same clarity of detailed development in Boyle as in Gilbert ; therefore we shall quote a paragraph, which seems to be a summary statement of the nature and function of this concept, from the works of Boyle : ' Not only the air, by reason of its thinness and subtility, is capable of being thus penetrated, moved, and altered, by these planetary virtues and lights ; but forasmuch also as our *spirits*, and the *spirits* likewise of all mixed bodies, are really of an *aerious, ethereal, luminous production*, and *composition* ; these spirits therefore of ours, and the spirits of all other bodies, must necessarily no less suffer an impression from the same lights, and cannot be less subject to an alteration, motion, agitation, and infection through them and by them, than the other, viz. the air : but rather as our *spirits* are more near and more analogous to the nature of light than the air, so they must be more prone and easy to be impressed than it. And if our *spirits*, and the *spirits* of all mixed bodies, may be altered, changed, moved and impressed by these superior bodies, and their properties ; then these *spirits being the only principles of energy, power, force, and life, in all bodies wherein they are, and the immediate causes through which all alteration comes to the bodies themselves ; it is impossible therefore spirits should be altered and changed,*[1] and yet no alteration made in the bodies themselves : and therefore a less limit or extreme cannot be set to the power or operation, or force of the superior bodies upon the inferior, than what must terminate at length into the very bodies themselves . . . as the sun shining on the rest of the planets doth not . . . only barely illuminate their bodies ; but besides this . . . [a body] . . . is not only enlightened, warmed, cherished and fructified, by the power, virtue, and influence of the sun, but hath its proper magnetical planetary virtue also fermented, stirred, agitated and awakened in it, which it remits back with the reflected light of the sun. . . .' [2]

§ II

Not only has Newton used the concepts of ' ethereal spirits ' or ' effluvia ' like his predecessors, but we find also his disciples employing the hypothesis of ' immaterial spirits or principles ' ; Newton commending their ability to expound and

[1] All italics are ours.
[2] *The General History of the Air, op. cit.*, vol. v, p. 641.

defend him correctly.[1] Therefore, from a brief study of two of his important followers, i. e. Richard Bentley and Samuel Clarke,[2] we shall be able to see better what Newton had in mind when he used these metaphysical categories.

Bentley, in his sermons, pointed out at great length [3] that mutual attraction and repulsion of bodies, without contact or impulse, cannot be attributed to mere matter, that it must be due to an immaterial cause—and that would be another argument for the being of God—' being a direct and positive proof that an immaterial living mind must inform and actuate the dead matter, and support the frame of the world '. Now if matter can act upon matter only by mutual contact—and that does not take place, as is known from actual experience—then it remains that the phenomena of gravity are produced ' either by the intervention of air or ether, or other such medium, that communicates the impulse from one body to another, or by effluvia and spirits, that are emitted from the one and pervene to the other '. In order to conceive *mechanically* that one particle attracts

---

[1] Brewster's *Memoirs*, vol. ii, p. 287 ; see also vol. ii, p. 287, foot-note 4.

[2] Bentley and Clarke, being divines, naturally adopt this speculative side of Newton's philosophy because it, better than any other aspect, lends itself admirably to their theistic doctrines.

[3] Bentley, *Sermons*, vol. vii, pp. 148 ff.

another by means of an impulse or agitation through ether—supposing that to be the case—then every single particle would have, by means of impulse or material effluvium, to agitate each and every other single particle in the whole universe ; and in order that that may take place we should have to imagine every particle sending its impulse or material effluvium in every direction at every moment of its agitation, or, in other words, Bentley thinks, every particle or physical point of matter would have to ' move all manner of ways equally and constantly ', which is absolutely impossible. Therefore we must affirm—says Bentley—' *that universal gravitation,* a thing certainly existent in nature, *is above all mechanism and material causes, and proceeds from a higher principle, a divine energy and impression* ', although its routine *may be described in mechanical terms.*[1]

Again, Clarke tells us explicitly that attraction and impulse have nothing in common with matter. Gravity cannot be explained by mutual impulsive attraction of matter, because every impulse acts in proportion to the surface, while gravity acts in direct proportion to the mass of a body. Consequently, there must be a principle which can get inside of a solid and hard body, and—*because attraction at a distance is absurd*—therefore we

[1] Bentley, *op. cit.*, vol. iii, pp. 163–5 ; the italics are ours.

must postulate *a certain immaterial spirit, which governs matter according to well ordered rules.* This immaterial force is universal in bodies, everywhere and always. As Clarke emphatically put it, ' Gravity or the weight of Bodies is not any accidental Effect of Motion or of any very subtile Matter, but an original and general Law of all Matter impressed upon it by God, and maintained in it perpetually by some efficient power, which penetrates the solid Substance of it. . . . Wherefore we ought no more to inquire how Bodies gravitate than how Bodies began first to be moved. It also follows that there is really a Vacuum in Nature.' [1]

But Bentley and Clarke went farther in their explanation of Newton than Newton himself would go. They took Newton's suggestion of a metaphysical cause of gravity as a hypothesis of physics, thus combining the fields of metaphysics or theology with that of science. Newton, on the other hand, as will be seen in Chapter V, made a distinction between the explanation of motion in terms of mechanical cause and a theological explanation in which motion is ultimately due to divine action.

[1] Rohault's *System of Natural Philosophy, illustrated with Dr. Samuel Clarke's Notes ; taken mostly out of Sir Isaac Newton's Philosophy* ; London, Knapton, 1723, vol. ii, p. 96 (Part II, chapter xxviii, Note 12) ; in the original Latin text, p. 573.

We may summarize our discussion to this point of the concept of ethereal spirits or effluvia as held by Newton and his predecessors. As we have seen, Gilbert used the notion in the field of magnetic and electrical action, while Boyle extended the use of effluvia, in an attempt to explain all types of attraction and repulsion. Newton, in many ways like Boyle, used the notion of ethereal spirits to explain many electrical, physiological, and magnetic phenomena. Here Newton aimed to suggest a mechanical explanation of motion just like Gilbert and Boyle before him. He did not confuse it with a theological explanation, as did his exponents—Bentley and Clarke. A further knowledge of Newton's notion of universal principles of motion may be gained from the study of his forerunners in *philosophy*— principally Boehme and More—as contrasted with the above study of his predecessors in *science*. In this study we shall be able to see Newton's attempt at a teleological explanation of gravity, which really supplies a necessary hypothesis for philosophy in general, or theology, just as the mechanical hypothesis of ethereal spirits just discussed was an attempt to fill the necessary gap for science.

§ III

Newton was directly influenced by Jacob Boehme's mysticism. As Brewster records,[1] Newton was a constant reader and admirer of Boehme, copying many a page from this, the greatest of Protestant mystic writers. Boehme's ideas about the cause of change in nature were important elements of this mystical doctrine as developed, principally by Henry More, who also directly influenced Newton.

For Boehme, ' quality ' as a ' mobility, boiling, springing, and driving of a thing ', has the same dynamic power and function as the ' ethereal spirit ' ; that is, God is known to men by his eternal nature in the unceasing action of seven ' forms ' or ' spirits ', which are the principles of the universe and of all life. Of these ' forms ', three are important for our consideration. The first form is conceived ' as astringence, hardness, coldness ; it is self-centredness '. The second form ' is motion, perception . . . the sting, the feeling, the principle, of dissatisfaction or unrest '. The third form arises from the other two, and is

---

[1] Brewster, *Memoirs*, vol. ii, p. 371. Newton has also studied Flamsteed's *Explication of Hierogliphic Figures* and W. Yworth's *Processus Mysterii Magni Philosophicus*. For Newton's controversies with Flamsteed in 1705-12 see Baily, *Life of Flamsteed*.

conceived as ' anguish wandering strain '.[1]   If we
were to express the above in modern terms we
should say that all change in the physical universe
before self-consciousness was developed is due to
the interplay of three forces, namely : (1) rest
or repulsion, (2) motion, involving attraction, and
(3) tension.

Henry More, who combined the teaching of
Boehme and of the Cabbala, exerted a great
influence upon the men of this day, particularly
at Cambridge, being himself a Fellow at Christ's
College. That the opinions of More were influen-
tial can be observed in the comments and references
made by Boyle ; also in Boyle's lengthy correspondence with More, especially in his reference to
More's criticism of Descartes's physics.[2]   Not only
did the Cambridge scholars value More's writings,
but the important philosophers on the continent
did also, for example Descartes, who was involved
in a lengthy correspondence with him.[3]   Therefore it is very possible that Newton was influenced
also by More, and, among other things, by his concept of gravitational attraction.

[1] *Aurora*, i. 4, and Penny's *Studies in Boehme*, London, 1912,
p. 151.

[2] *Hydrostatical Discourse, occasioned by the objections of
learned Dr. Henry More, op. cit.*, vol. iii, p. 596, pp. 601 ff. ;
see also vol. vi, pp. 512–15.

[3] For Descartes's correspondence with More see Cousin's
edition of Descartes's *Works*, vol. ix.

More cites a large number of reasons for the existence of an immaterial force, of which the following are important examples :

(1) The nature of gravity points to the fact that the phenomena of nature are not mere functions of ' Mechanical Powers of Matter ' ; e. g. we can imagine how much force is necessary to exert upon a lead bullet in order for it ' to recede from superficies of the Earth, the Bullet being in so swift a Motion as would dispatch some fifteen Miles in one Minute of an Hour ; it must needs appear that a wonderful Power is required to curb it, regulate it, or remand it back to the Earth, and keep it there, notwithstanding the strong Reluctancy of that first Mechanical Law of Matter that would urge it to recede. Whereby is manifested not only the marvellous Power of *Unity* and *Indiscerptibility in* the *Spirit of Nature*, but that there is a peremptory and even forcible Execution of an *all-comprehensive and eternal Counsel* for the *ordering* and the *guiding* of the Motion of *Matter* in the Universe to what is for the *Best*. And this phenomenon of Gravity is of so *good* and *necessary* consequence, that there could be neither Earth, nor Inhabitants without it, in this State that things are.' [1]

[1] *An Antidote Against Atheism,* London, 1717, Book II, chap. ii, Article 7 ; see also *The Immortality of the Soul,* London, 1718, Preface, p. xii.

(2) Matter, being a simple homogeneous substance, must have throughout the same primary properties ; and therefore it must be either without motion, or else be self-moving, its motion being of the same kind and velocity. But if it be shown that bodies move at different velocities, then the cause of it must lie outside of matter. But if matter is devoid of motion, then it is plain that motion is due to some other substance which is not matter, but rather a *Substance Incorporeal*. But if bodies be moved by themselves, in a definite measure, the effect must be an ' emanative ' one,[1] especially if there be no ' external impediment '. But if the ' Planets had but a common Dividend of all the Motion which themselves, and the Sun and Stars and all the Ethereal Matter possess (the matter of Planets being so little in comparison of that of the Sun, Stars, and Ether) the proportion of Motion that will fall due to them would be exceeding much above what they have. . . . Wherefore, every Planet could not fail of melting itself into little less finer Substance than the purest Ether.' And because they are not melting into fine fragments is a proof that they have no motion or agitation in themselves. Consequently the

---

[1] More puts down as an axiom the following : ' An Emanative Effect is coexistent with the very Substance of that which is said to be the cause thereof.' *Immortality of the Soul*, Axiom 17, p. 18.

motion of matter is due to outside principles, and
these are not material.[1] ' *Nam sic Mobilia omnia
moventur a Deo* '.[2]

(3) There are other happenings in nature which
demand spiritual causes, because natural ones
cannot explain them, and these are ' speaking,
knockings, opening of Doors when they are fast
shut, sudden lights in the midst of a room floating
in the air, and then passing and vanishing ; nay
shapes of men and several sort of Brutes, that,
after speech and converse, have suddenly dis-
appeared '.[3]

(4) If we consider the ' transcendent excellency
of the Nature of God ', who is a Being perfect in
every way, this points to the necessary existence of
an immaterial substance, because God, being perfect, cannot be a material body.   And God being
an extended Being, for He is omnipresent, spiritual
substance must have the attribute of extension.[4]

The function of this ' immaterial cause ' is
various, according to More.   By penetrating
matter, it is the source of motion, of cohesion, or
separation of parts of bodies, it is the directing

[1] *Immortality of the Soul*, Book I, chap. xi, Arts. 2, 3, pp. 40–1.
[2] *Enchiridion Metaphysicum, sive de Rebus Incorporeis*, London,
Flesher, 1671, p. 380 (Part I, chap. xxviii, Article 3).
[3] *Immortality of the Soul*, p. 47 (Book I, chap. xviii, Art. 1).
[4] *Ibid.*, p. 40 (Book I, chap. xi, Article 1).

force of all motion, and the source of animal and human locomotion, &c.[1] We may notice the similarity of function assigned to this spiritual principle by More and Newton, and in fact by all the men discussed in this chapter.

The characteristic properties of this immaterial substance, says More, are penetrability, indiscerptibility, extension, and activity;[2] it is intrinsically endowed with life, for material extension without life would be destitute of all motion. Spiritual substance is attributed by More to God, the Angels, the mind of man, and to space.[3]

It is this spiritual essence that is responsible for the change and the motion in the universe, says More. By admitting the existence of matter in corpuscular form, which is moved by outside forces or spirits according to mathematically expressed laws—that is with geometrical uniformity—he comes close to a kinetic theory of motion, as did Newton. With this concept of the function of metaphysical causes he did not need to abolish the mechanical or mathematical laws of motion. He explains these laws in terms only

---

[1] *Immortality of the Soul*, pp. 26 ff. (Book I, chap. vii).

[2] *Ibid.*, pp. 5, 6 (Book I, chap. ii, Art. 11, 12); see also *Enchiridion Metaphysicum*, p. 379.

[3] *Enchiridion Metaphysicum*, chap. xxviii, par. 2, p. 377; par. 3, p. 378; par. 7, 384; see also chap. viii.

of metaphysical causes. More was a great lover
of Descartes's philosophy, but he could not sub-
scribe to Descartes's doctrine that the cause of
motion is a material and mechanical one, an impact of solid bodies. If Descartes's impact-
motion is a true explanation of change, then there
would be nothing left for God to do. Furthermore, More asks Descartes : If the world is filled
with matter, where would he put God? Descartes
answered that the infinity attributed to God does
not consist in ' being extended everywhere ', but
rather in His infinity of power. More replied that
infinity of power is a mode of God's very essence ;
therefore God is everywhere.[1] It is because of
God's extension that he can freely move matter,
More thought ; he created the world and certain
laws which are mechanical. So he might say
mechanism is an aspect of nature, but things in
nature cannot be explained fully by mere mechanical relationships. The whole world, More believed, is pervaded by spirit ; this spirit is not God
himself, but rather the spirit of nature of *anima
mundi*.[2] As he says, ' it is a substance incorporeal
but without sense and animadversion,' acting
upon matter as a ' plastic power raising such

[1] Letters, More to Descartes, Cousin's edition of Descartes's
Works, vol. ix, pp. 178 ff.
[2] Preface to the *Immortality of the Soul.*

phenomena in the world by directing the paths of the matter and their motion, as cannot be resolved into mere mechanical powers'[1] or general mathematical laws. Spiritual and material substance being both extended, the one can act directly upon the other. This spiritual power, the *anima mundi*, says More, acts upon the bodies not by penetrating them but by extending itself over the bodies, by expanding or contracting without losing any of its essence or power, while the density of matter can only be changed by a separation or combination which is purely mechanical in nature. Material and spiritual bodies can exist in the same place at the same time. It is by the recognition that space is filled with spirit, and in fact that space is spirit extended over all things, that the gap between God and matter is bridged. As More says : space is not only something real but something divine ; in fact it represents to us the divine essence. '*Est confusior quaedam et generalior repraesentatio essentiae, sive essentialis praesentiae divinae quatenus a vita atque operationibus praeciditur.*'[2]

The same concept of space appears in Newton. Space and time are natural realities for Newton ;

[1] *Immortality of the Soul*, chap. xii.

[2] *Enchiridion Metaphysicum*, 1671, Part I, chap. viii, par. 15, p. 74 ; see *Immortality of the Soul*, Preface, p. 12.

they are homogeneous ; the one is tridimensional,
the other onedimensional, and mathematical in
character.[1] As has been pointed out in Chapter I,
Newton made a distinction between absolute and
relative space, the opposition is the same as that
of the mathematical, geometrical, or rational
structure of the universe to that which is sensible.
Indeed, absolute and relative space are the same
as mathematical and the sensible.[2] Newton did
not use the concept of absolute space to any
great advantage in his mathematical physics. As
Mach says : ' Newton's use of absolute space in
the development of the law of inertia is quite
unnecessary, in fact " the law of inertia does not
involve absolute space " '.[3] We must remember

[1] Gassendi thought of space and time as being things *sui
generis*, neither being mere quality. Galileo was the first one to
point out that absolute space, which is the immovable supporter
of all material objects, is not an object of sensuous perception.

[2] *Principia*, 1729, vol. i, p. 9 ; ' Absolute space, in its own
nature, without regard to anything external, remains always
similar and immovable. Relative space is some movable dimension or measure of the absolute space ; which our sense deter-
mines by its position to bodies ; and which is vulgarly taken for
immovable spaces ; such is the dimension of a subterraneous, and
aereal, or celestial space, determined by its position in respect of
earth. . . .' See also *Optics*, 3rd ed., Qu. 28. That position was
not understood by the Cartesians ; e. g. for Leibniz space is
something purely ideal, it is a collection of all abstract possible
relations.

[3] *Science of Mechanics*, trans. by McCormick, Chicago, 2nd ed.,
pp. 235–6.

that at that time Newtonian mechanics, as we know it to-day, did not exist. What, then, is the metaphysical function of absolute space?

Newton says in the twenty-eighth query to the third edition of the *Optics* that it appears from natural phenomena 'that there is a Being, incorporeal, living, intelligent, omnipresent, who, in infinite Space, as it were in his Sensory, sees the things themselves intimately, and thoroughly perceives them, and comprehends them wholly by their immediate presence to himself. . . .' Again, in the thirty-first query, Newton continues: 'A powerful ever-living Agent, who, being in all Places, is more able by his will to move the Bodies within his boundless uniform Sensorium, and thereby to form and reform the Parts of the Universe. . . . And yet we are not to consider the World as the Body of God, or the several Parts thereof, as the Parts of God.' [1] Such a consideration might lead to Pantheism.

Clarke, explaining to Leibniz the function of Newtonian space, said: 'God perceives everything, not by *means* of any *Organ*, but by being *himself* actually present everywhere. This *everywhere*, therefore, or *universal Space*, is the *Place* of his *Perception*.' [2]

[1] *Optics*, 3rd ed., p. 379.
[2] *Correspondence between Leibniz and Clarke*, p. 323; see also pp. 3 and 13.

From the above quotations it is clear that Newton attributed to ' Space ' an important function, i. e. that of being the medium through which God can come in contact with finite objects and creatures, if it be not actual sensorium of God ; though Clarke claimed that space is not an actual ' organ of sense ' but rather God's being ' everywhere ' ; and this ' everywhere ' is space ; that is, he identifies the extension of God with Space. God being infinitely extended, and having a Being in itself and for itself, that is, having existence independent of any other existing being, then space, being a ' sensorium ' or the ' divine extension ', must also have the characteristic of ' absolute reality ' and must be infinitely extended.

In More's work and Newton's we have found the same metaphysical function attributed to space. In the conception of space of both we have the contact point of material bodies with spiritual forces. But Newton, as a mathematician, added a mathematic element to his conception. It is in the law of gravitation through the action at a distance which is a mathematical expression of an empirical fact—which is not by material impact nor action through a material medium—that Newton found a mathematical and empirical conformation of More's Neo-Platonic philosophy. While action at a distance, as such, is impossible to conceive, it becomes possible, however, if we accept the notion that space is the non-material medium of attraction. God acting through that medium, makes gravitational motion possible. This action is not mechanical; however, it is orderly, direct, and immediate.[1]

The influence upon Newton of a philosophy of the type so ably represented by More is to be seen again in Newton's objection to the doctrine that the world is a machine. Because Newton's metaphysical notions of gravity can be more clearly understood in the light of his objections to a ' world machine '—a concept just touched upon in Chapter II—we will now sketch this important doctrine. It was Archimedes who suggested a mechanical conception of nature. Da Vinci, Kepler, and Galileo thought nature to be geometrical, but it was Descartes who is responsible for a consistent development of the universe in terms of a machine. Newton, however, used the concept of nature as a machine in the science of physics, while in metaphysics, or theology, that notion had no place. Descartes

[1] *Principia*, book I, sect. xi, prop. 69, scholium. It may be of interest to note that Kant was influenced by Newton as regards his notion of space. And earlier, after Locke had accepted much of Newton, Berkeley opposed the absolute reality of space, as leading to materialism and atheism, and this apparently with Newton's opinions prominently in mind.

aimed to explain motion and change by means of mechanical causes. This mechanism was a result of reason ; he never thought that science must be based only upon the results of experimental facts. Descartes developed his mechanics from a set of metaphysical axioms. That the order of the universe is geometrical was accepted by Newton as it was by Descartes, but for different reasons ; he even gave a different meaning to this order. For Descartes, God is only the efficient cause of motion, the geometrical relations and the uniformity of nature is due to God's perfection. Newton thought that this regularity is an actual and direct product of God's activity, residing in a providential arrangement, freely imposed upon the world ; and this arrangement is geometrical.[1] Furthermore, the cause of celestial regularity, Newton thought, is not mechanical, because if it were we should find more uniformity than is actually found. A Cartesian or Leibnizian world-machine could never explain nature, Newton thought. Irregularities which have arisen in nature, e. g. the irregularities in our solar system, due to the reciprocal action of planets and comets upon one another, presuppose the constant intervention of God, who regulates, as the emergency arises, the motion of these heavenly bodies.

[1] *Optics*, 3rd ed. , Qu. 31.

Newton believed that this alone, if nothing else, points to the necessary existence of God. The regularity of the universe—shown in its being mathematically expressible—is another proof for a providential order.[1] As Newton said, referring to the cause of gravity, ' this is certain, that it must proceed from a cause that penetrates to the very centres of the sun and planets, without suffering the least diminution in its force; [which is contrary to the laws of mechanics] that operates not according to the quantity of the surfaces of the particles upon which it acts (as mechanical causes used to do), but according to the quantity of the solid matter which they contain, and propagates its virtues on all sides. . . .' [2]

Clarke, defending Newton's philosophy and criticizing Leibniz's pre-established harmony,

---

[1] *Principia*, at the end of Book III, General Scholium. Leibniz also thought that it was the diversity of things that points to the necessary existence of God. Laplace and Lagrange have shown that these planetary irregularities are periodical and equalize one another, though minor ones still remain unexplained.

[2] *Mathematical Principles of Natural Philosophy*, 1713 ed., pp. 483–4 ; see also Cotes's preface to the 2nd ed. (last three pages). Newton's letters to Bentley ; also in the 3rd ed. of the *Optics* ; in these letters to Bentley, Newton speaks of the possibility of God's creating different forces, ' *thereby to vary the laws of Nature*, and make worlds of several sorts in several parts of the universe ' (pp. 378–80) ; which would be impossible—as we may add—if the structure of the world should be mechanistic.

said also, ' The notion of the world's being a great machine, going on without the interposition of God, as a clock continues to go without the assistance of a clockmaker, is the notion of material- ism and fate, and tends to exclude Providence and God's government in reality out of the world.' [1] And in another place, he said : ' The means by which two bodies attract each other may be *invisible* and intangible, and of a different nature from *mechanism* ; and yet, acting regularly and constantly, may well be called natural.' [2]

Bentley developed the same ideas in his sermons,[3] which Newton heartily approved.[4] But the greatness of Newton as a scientist is in this : that he never admitted—as did most of his followers, e.g. Clarke and Bentley—the legitimacy of scientific recourse to such a metaphysical sup- plementary postulate ; or that the foundation of science should rest directly upon metaphysical axioms, as the Cartesians believed.

[1] *Collection of Papers, &c.*, Leibniz and Clarke, p. 15.

[2] Cf. *ibid.*, p. 151 ; see also p. 351.

[3] Bentley, vol. iii. especially Sermon VII.

[4] Bentley, *op. cit.*, vol. iii, pp. 152 ff. More, in his criticism of Descartes, because of the latter's mechanistic theory of the universe, defends the doctrine that mechanism is not a meta- physical explanation ; in fact, by the pure laws of mechanics we could never explain gravity (*Immortality of the Soul*, Preface, p. 12 ; also *Enchiridion Metaphysicum*, chap. xi).

Newton, like many men of his day, accepted the belief in the existence of God, dogmatically, sentimentally, passionately. He fought against atheism and materialism at all costs. For Newton no opposition between religion and science existed, any more than between faith and knowledge. The opposition between religion and science really belongs to a later generation of men. Religious problems to Newton were problems of exposition and apologetics.

As has been indicated, Newton's dogmatic belief in God involved the conception that the attributes of God are geometrical—eternity and infinity—and absolute space and time become divine attributes of nature.

We may now summarize Newton's doctrine of God and his relation to the world of motion. Newton wanted to explain gravity in terms of final and immaterial causes. He sought an explanation of the nature of Being in categories that were not at all *anti-scientific* but which rather—as in any scientific description—make for the order and regularity of nature. All these categories have geometrical attributes, and consequently nature can be described scientifically in terms of mathematics and mechanics. That is, God acts directly and regularly upon nature ; His presence is everywhere, substantially and throughout all eternity. He is the first cause and source of all motion and change. His influence is direct, not only upon matter, but direct also in the influence of matter upon mind and mind upon matter. In this respect mechanical laws do not hold true— the equality of action and reaction fails, because the divine principle does not lose or gain in its activity. In absolute space there is a contact point of material bodies with spiritual forces, which contact is *not* by impact nor through a material medium. The action, as it is described by the law of gravitation, is *direct* and *immediate* in the form of immaterial ethereal emanations of *spiritual* forces through absolute space as its medium, which space is in itself an immaterial ' Sensorium of God '. As man has a consciousness which is his sensorium of action, so God has a soul which is space. But as ' God needs no particular organ to operate ' as the human soul does, God and His divine sensorium are the same. God becomes the ' Soul of the World ', being immediately substantially present everywhere—although Newton tried to guard himself against Pantheism. But God being the soul of the world, dominates the world completely ; matter and man alike are subject to His domination.[1]

---

[1] *Principia*, Gen. Schol., also *Optics*, 3rd ed., Qu. 28, see also *Collection of Papers . . . Leibniz and Clarke*, p. 15. The

While the motion of matter follows the general laws of mechanics, the real or final Cause of motion does not, but a Divine Providence creates, conserves, and regulates motion, in order that ' bodies may not go off their course '.

The relation of mathematics and physics to philosophy in general or theology, which has been touched upon throughout this discussion, will be discussed in the next chapter.

same tendency is to be found in other thinkers of his day—Malebranche, Fénelon, certain tendencies in Leibniz, and also among the Neo-Platonists. As Bloch points out, this submission of creatures to the will and power of their Creator is the basis of a natural theology for Newton. The basis is not to be found in reason, but in feeling, sentiment, and intuition. We can know God only by His actions, by His attributes ; we can never gain a direct, real, and true knowledge of Him, as Descartes and Spinoza thought we could. *La Philosophie de Newton* by Léon Bloch, Paris, 1908, pp. 515–16.

THE ROLE OF MATHEMATICS and HYPOTHESIS in NEWTON'S PHYSICS

THE distinction between philosophy in general and theology on the one hand, and experimental philosophy or science on the other, which was pre-supposed in the discussions of the above chapters, will be clearly understood in the light of Newton's notions of scientific method in general, which is connected with his conceptions about the function that mathematics plays in science, and finally the nature and place of hypothesis. While we discuss the role of mathematics in physics it will be possible to state our general conclusions about Newton's ideas with regard to atoms and mecha-nism. Our study of the nature and function of scientific laws also enable us to state our general conclusions about the nature and function of Newton's universal law of gravity, while our study of Newton's use of hypothesis will enable us to state our final conclusions about his hypothesis of gravity. Consequently we will first discuss Newton's forerunners in scientific method;

second, the role of mathematics in physics; third, the relation of science to metaphysics; fourth and finally, the nature and function of hypothesis.

Da Vinci in the fifteenth century laid stress on the significance of experience. Our knowledge acquires perfect certainty by means of the employment of mathematics, he pointed out, saying that mathematical deductions are necessary deductions, and one of the rules of nature is necessity.[1] The importance of mathematical deduction and proof was regarded very highly even as late as the early eighteenth century, as may be seen from the following quotation from Huygens, referring to his proof of the wave theory of light : ' One finds in this subject a kind of [experimental] demonstration which does not carry with it so high a degree of certainty as that employed in geometry ; and which differs distinctly from the method employed by geometers in that they prove their propositions by well-established and incontrovertible principles, which principles, while here experimental principles, are tested by the inferences which are derivable from them. The nature of the subject permits of no other treatment. It is possible, however, in this way to

[1] Höffding, H. A., *History of Modern Philosophy*, trans. Meyer, London, 1915, vol. i, p. 165.

establish a probability, which is little short of certainty. . . .' [1]

Galileo also stressed the necessity of mathematical demonstration. Only in mathematics does the opposition between immediate perception and knowledge disappear to a large degree, he thought, because in mathematics the human mind participates in the necessity with which God thinks the truths which underlie nature. By mathematical or geometrical deductions Galileo had not in mind formal logic, such as that of Aristotle. As he said : ' Logic, it appears to me, teaches us how to test the conclusiveness of any argument or demonstration. . . .', [2] but does not give us the knowledge to be tested. Galileo, like Pascal, turned to mathematical interpretations of experience as a source of knowledge. Galileo showed the dependence of physical science upon mathematics, but he was not interested in mathematical science as such. 'True philosophy expounds nature to us : but she can be understood only by him who has learned the speech and symbols in which she speaks to us. This speech is mathematics, and its symbols are mathematical figures. . . .' By

[1] Newton, Sir Isaac, *Principia*, trans. by A. Motte, London, 1729, Preface, p. 4.

[2] Galilei, Galileo, *Two New Sciences*, trans. by Crew and de Salvio, Macmillan, 1914, p. 138.

philosophy he means science as much as meta-physics, and for him philosophy rested upon empirical facts which give us the causes in nature, and these are put in mathematical symbols by 'philosophers', thus giving us the form and relationship of things, nature being geome-trical.

Galileo's scientific method may be described briefly in the following way. The first step is the making of definitions and axioms. These must not be arbitrary ; they must be true of nature ; that is, their truth must be experimentally deter-mined. These definitions should be common and easy.[1] It is by the use of reason or by mathe-matics that we deduce further knowledge from these simple definitions ; this is the second step.[2] So the analytic and synthetic methods are com-plementary. In using this method, Galileo, like Kepler before him, felt that the laws of nature would be found by the analysis of the facts of experience plus the co-ordinations of these results in mathematical generalizations.

Newton followed in the footsteps of Da Vinci, Kepler, and Galileo. He, like Galileo before him, pointed out the function that mathematics must

[1] Galileo, *Two New Sciences*, trans. by Crew and de Salvio, Macmillan, 1914, pp. 160–2.

[2] *Ibid.*, pp. 162–4.

play in the discovery of secondary causes. Newton believed mathematical formulas expressing general laws of experimental physics must not rest upon axioms which are derived *a priori* ; they must be a result of experience ; they must be generalizations from patterns, of nature furnished to us by our experience of facts, whether it be in the street or laboratory. Newton showed by example that we must first analyse facts of experience in order to construct our pattern, which can be synthesized when mathematically developed. The axioms or definitions are results of analysis (Mathematical analysis) which when connected systematically (mathematical synthesis) give rise to new generalizations (due to mathematical deduction), in turn giving rise to new discoveries of physical facts. The truth of these generalizations is directly dependent upon our constant guidance by experience in our procedure.

It would be fallacious to think, however, that mathematics adapts itself to physics, any more than algebra adapts itself to geometry and gives rise to analytical geometry. The fact is that mathematical physics is the true physics, a fact recognized by Newton. For Newton, mathematical physics is not in any sense opposed to experimental physics ; the former is the *ideal* towards which all development of experimental physics should tend. All experiments are means which lead to mathematical explanation ; that is actually the true function of mathematics in physics in the mind of Newton. It is the experiment which gives value or truth to experimental physics, but in its perfect and most useful form it is expressed in mathematical language, and consequently the fact of experimental physics becomes the fact of mathematical physics.[1]

[Therefore Newton was convinced that the role of mathematics in physics is not that of a discipline independent of facts, and that mathematics does *not* give us *truth a priori*. All mathematical physics must begin with facts of experience. To explain fully what Newton meant by truth in this connexion would necessitate a discussion of the relation of physics to metaphysics, which will be developed below.[2] The exact role of mathematics in Newton's Natural Philosophy

[1] Newton, *Mathematical Principles of Natural Philosophy*, English translation by A. Motte, 1st ed., London, 1729, vol. i, p. 262.

[2] We may point out briefly in this connexion, what is now generally agreed, that it is due to Newton's doctrine of symmetry and not to the Leibnizian principle of sufficient reason that prediction in science is possible, and that truth in physics is intelligible. It is because of the symmetry in the objects of experience themselves that we can rightfully expect a symmetry of effect from a given cause, and not because of the existence of a rational order of principles which guarantees deduction.

is not to establish mathematical science or
mathematical theorems; no more is it to establish *a priori* connexion between different facts.
These could be known empirically. The role of
mathematics is to make the connexion more easily
obtainable and to serve to discover and to express
laws, not to prove them, much less than that to
prove that they have an eternal value. The pre-
Newtonian syllogistic physics has nothing in
common with the mathematical physics of Newton.
As Newton says in the Preface to the *Principia* of
1687 : ' Therefore geometry is founded in mechanical practice, and is nothing but that part of
universal mechanics which accurately proposes and
demonstrates the art of measuring.' Further, in
the Preface he says the following : ' Therefore
we offer this work as the mathematical principles
of philosophy : for all the difficulty of philosophy
seems to consist in this . . . from the phenomena
of motion to investigate the forces of nature, and
then from these forces to demonstrate the other
phenomena ; and to this end the general propositions in the first and second books are directed.
In the third book we give an example of this
in the explication of the System of the World :
for by the propositions mathematically demonstrated in the former books, we in the third,
derive from the celestial phenomena the forces of

gravity with which bodies tend to the sun and the several planets. Then from these forces, by other propositions which are also mathematical we deduce the motion of the planets, the comets, the moon, and the sea.' And again, Newton wrote in the introduction to the third book of his *Principia* : ' In the preceding Books I have laid down the principles of philosophy : principles not philosophical, but mathematical ; such, to wit, as we may build our reasoning upon in philosophical inquiries. These principles are the laws and conditions of certain motions, and powers or forces which chiefly have respect to philosophy ; but lest they should have appeared of themselves dry and barren, I have illustrated them here and there with some philosophical scholium. . . .'

The precise distinction between mathematics and physics, as Newton conceived it, will be clarified by the following consideration. Newton asked ' If the virtue of any particle diffuse itself every way *ad infinitum* there will be required a greater force to produce equal condensation of a greater quantity of the fluid. But whether elastic fluids do really consist of particles so repelling each other, is a physical question. We have here demonstrated mathematically the property of fluids consisting of particles of this kind, that hence philosophers may take occasion to discuss the question.' [1] That is, Newton was certain of the existence of elastic particles, but he was not certain of the mathematical deductions that follow —that is, whether these particles actually repel each other was a physical fact or not. The only way to know this would be to verify the deductions experimentally.

The force of the above distinction—mathematical deductions and physical facts—becomes significant when we are reminded that it was Newton's conception of particles or atoms as mathematically demonstrated that became so fundamental to all future mechanics. Newton, like Galileo before him, thought that the fundamental properties of matter are those only which lend themselves to quantitative treatment. As has been pointed out above, mathematical theory is the result of patterns constructed from physical facts of experience, and, if this mathematical theory is developed, it gives rise to generalizations which give rise to new ideas, when mastered by physicists. These ideas lead to new discoveries, and finally change or develop the original pattern. Consequently, it was natural for Newton, as well as for any other physicist, to develop a mathe-

[1] Newton, Sir Isaac, *Mathematical Principles of Natural Philosophy*, English translation by A. Motte, 1st ed., London, 1729, vol. ii, p. 79.

matical theory based upon the quantitative properties of matter, which alone lend themselves
to mathematical treatment.

Therefore, when forces are conceived as Newton
conceived them, as applied to each particle of
a solid, they may also be conceived as applied
to a point of the solid called its centre of gravity.
The summation of these forces in a single point
is called by Newton a centripetal force, to which
he gave a mathematical expression, actually a
natural development of Kepler's laws. Newton
defined force in terms of algebra, as an expression
of an element in movement measures in an
element of time. Force and space for Newton
are in functional relationship, which is scientifically expressed in mathematical terms. Movement is associated with force, and force is a
mathematical concept of a physical, natural
fact. It was Galileo who gave Newton the idea of
force, and the idea that gravity exists in a field
of such forces, upon which pattern Newton
constructed his mathematical equation.[1] It is
very natural for a mathematical physicist to conceive of a body as made up of physical particles
between which certain internal actions of forces
are constantly working ; so that a body is reduced
to a system of points and forces. By doings this

[1] See above, Chapter II.

the problem of motion and equilibrium resolves itself into an application of the principles of mechanics of the particle. Or the forces of a body, in fact, resolve themselves into a summation of forces, as the force of a fixed or constant centre of gravity of a body. Within any such mass, particles or molecules have a geometrical characteristic which is constant no matter what force we may apply to them. This forms a system of physical static relations which are adaptable to mathematical treatment.[1]

[1] The reason why Newton or the scientists in general could make such assumptions is because natural science, e. g. physics or astronomy, deals with large aggregates of particles. The heterogeneity of relations which *may* actually exist between these particles is negligible, and a single simple mathematical expression of these relations is not only possible but very desirable because of its utility. For example, when we assert that an ellipsoid with a great number of dimensions can be defined sufficiently by five or six constants, we mean only that our study of mathematical theory, modelled after ellipsoids, can be expressed by means of these five or six constants. Mathematical theory, therefore, can be reduced to a small number of equations which involve a small number of constants, but it would be folly to say that the actual physical models are so simple in structure. We may notice another example of *ideal simplification*. When we express the rate of emission of the particle, which as a matter of fact it has been actually impossible to see with accuracy, what we really express is the *mean number*, and that is really the only thing that we have scientifically arrived at. Here physical facts are only *mean numbers*, and these are only the facts accessible to our observation.

We say that *A* is a function of *B* if *A* changes with *B*, and we

Newton's additional notions about scientific method become clearer when we discover the dis-

can calculate the derivative which will represent this rate of change. We say that this derivative represents the law or rate of change of the body, or, in other words, that this derivative stands for the relationship which exists between A and B. But if we carefully observe the change of A and B, whether it be in a physical, chemical, biological, or psychological laboratory, and plot the curve representing this functional change, we find that the relationship between A and B is not at all as absolute as the principle concept of calculus has it; in fact, the change plotted does not at all represent a curve. What we really have between our X and Y axes, as a fact of actual experience, is a number of points widely distributed, but yet within certain limits representing a continuously progressing curve. (For a further discussion see my paper 'Time and Speculative Philosophy', *Monist*, October 1919.)

Because the bodies and their motions studied by physicists are apparently so nearly homogeneous, it is therefore possible for them to employ mathematical generalizations of relations in order to express their behaviour and nature. It was necessary for Newton to assume that particles are homogeneous, and the pattern of nature based upon the pattern of experience dealt with lent themselves to that end. This was necessary, because if the particles (or atoms) were supposed to be heterogeneous, no mathematical or any other simple treatment of them would be possible. And, furthermore, it was not only necessary to admit the above generalizations, but also that the resultant action of a body would be the direct sum of the actions of all its parts, and that all bodies being made up on similar homogeneous atoms would behave alike. For a generalization contrary to the one stated above would not permit any single and simple equation summarizing the behaviour of matter, based on a large number of diverse facts. That is the reason why the statistical method as

tinctions that he made between science (natural philosophy) and metaphysics (philosophy in general). This is best seen against the background of Descartes's ideas, to which Newton objected. Descartes developed the doctrine of the geometrical characteristics of matter from a metaphysical point of view, whereas for Newton *purely* geo-

employed in science is so fruitful ; it always supplies to mathematics the indispensable ideal patterns, which are constructed on the basis of observable facts which really are the *mean numbers*.

Again, it is mathematical theory which can bring together under a single generalization the crude facts of isolated experience so different in types as, e.g. the motion of solid bodies, of light, of sound, or of matter.

If the main business of physics (or natural science in general) is to discover and describe the order characteristic of its subject-matter, to describe the past and predict the future with a certain amount of accuracy, then it is legitimate for physics (or science in general) to assume that bodies are functions of their minute units, and that the behaviour of a body is the resultant of or a function of the behaviour of its units, or that a number of isolated facts can be expressed by a single equation even though this mathematical equation be based upon an ideal pattern, arrived at by a *mean number* statistically derived from observed facts of nature.

It must be borne in mind, however, that these considerations did not play any part in Newton's ideas about the philosophy of science. (For a further discussion see my papers 'The Role of Mathematics in Physics', *Journal of Philosophy*, 21 July 1921, and ' Spinoza's Use of " Euclidean Form " of Exposition ', *Monist*, vol. 33, No. 3, 1923.)

See Enriques for an interesting attempt to translate Newtonian particles into the modern notion of electrons. *Problems of Science*, trans. by K. Royce, Open Court, Chicago, 1914, pp. 355 ff.

metrical qualities of matter—qualities considered
metaphysically—had no meaning, because the
properties are always physically and experimentally discovered. Shape or figure, impenetrability, volume, density, and all the other qualities
are physical qualities of matter, just as much as
heat or tension, said Newton, and are not merely
geometrical attributes of extension. It is impossible, Newton thought, to derive all of these
properties *a priori* from the mere configuration
of matter, much less to explain all physics from
the geometrical properties of matter. In fact,
there are very many properties of matter ; and
how many and what they are we shall know only
as we make progress in natural science. The
general belief of the time was that with the advance
of knowledge it would be possible to reduce, more
and more, the primary qualities of matter.
Newton believed, however, that with the advance
of knowledge we should come closer to a final
point of view—that of God, and He sees things in
more detail than we ever shall. While our knowledge is true as far as we have gone, nevertheless
there are many qualities of matter that we do not
know. The truth even of what is known about
secondary causes is limited, if by nothing else, by
the imperfection of our scientific instruments.

The above conviction of Newton logically

followed from his views about the relation of
science to philosophy in general. Newton thought
that all the sciences form a unity, which he called
natural philosophy. However, contrary to the
Cartesians, Newton claimed that it is not the
function of philosophy in general, as distinguished
from experimental philosophy, to justify the
axioms of science, nor did he believe that there
is any necessary continuity between science or
experimental philosophy on the one hand, and
philosophy in general and theology on the other.
The foundations of science rest upon experience
as much in Newton's opinion as in Kepler's
or Galileo's. Science should never begin with
final or first causes. Theology, which deals with
final causes, was thought by Newton to be based
not on an analysis of experience, but on direct
revelation, even though he believed experience
pointed to the same truths. Nevertheless, Newton
did not abruptly separate philosophy in general
from experimental or natural philosophy. The
philosophy dealing with the first and final causes,
though not at the head of science, is not outside of
it, in his opinion, but it is at the culmination of
science ; it is the result, and comes at the com-
pletion, of scientific knowledge. As Newton said
in the twenty-eighth question of his *Optics*,
' though every true step made in this natural

philosophy brings us *not* immediately to the Knowledge of the Cause, yet it brings us nearer to it.' The value of experimental philosophy to Newton was based on its being a true stepping-stone which may finally enable us to get to the true first cause. That does not mean that scientific knowledge does not give us the true (secondary) causes of nature, but rather that these are not the final and complete true causes.

Only when natural science is completed—that is, when all facts are known and correlated—Newton thought, will it yield us the final point of view, the final cause or the first principle which governs the universe. Only in the light of our knowledge about the ordering and regulating principles of the Universe, if we are to believe Newton, shall we be able properly to understand the significance of natural laws as they were derived by our fragmentary knowledge dealt with by science in its various stages of development. Thus the ordering principle of the universe in Divine Providence. Consequently Newton's conviction was that the first cause is not mechanical, nor is the operation of the moving spirits upon matter mechanical, e. g. the law of equality of action and reaction does not hold true. Mechanism, or even atomism, is not the goal of mathematical physics ; it is only one subordinate aspect of it. Physics, for Newton, as a science was more general.[1]

Thus philosophy not only explained for Newton the secondary causes, supplying the secondary natural laws, which are mechanical, but paved the way for the knowledge of the first cause, which is not mechanical. As is now clear, it was through tradition, or as it appeared to him, through revelation, that Newton obtained his conviction that there is a first cause and that this cause is a natural one but not mechanical, even though following mechanical laws of operation. The reason he was so cautious in employing that conviction in the explanation of gravity in his physics was that, first, he had no experimental confirmation of it, and, secondly, that a rational demonstration could be offered only when all natural science should be completed.[2] Also, that for Newton the first cause was not mechanical —that was the theoretical reason, or what might be better called the theological reason (conviction) for Newton's distrust of the attempts to ' finally '

[1] Newton, Sir Isaac, *Optics*, London, 1706 edition, Book II, Par. 3, Prop. 7, 8 ; Book III, Qu. 28.

[2] *Ibid.*, Qu. 28, 30, and 31, and Newton, Sir Isaac, *Mathematical Principles of Natural Philosophy*, English translation by A. Motte, 1st ed., London, 1729 ; General Scholium, at the end of Book III.

explain the universe in terms of atomistic mechanism.

The same opposition was felt by Newton regarding the Cartesian interpretation of the nature and function of scientific laws. Are the laws developed by mathematical physics real, or do they only approach the real causes which are not fundamentally mathematical nor mechanical? The Cartesians thought that mathematical science would give us *a priori* the real and absolutely true laws of nature, while experience should be used only to verify them. The reason we can never completely verify these laws, they said, is not that they are not perfect, but rather because of the imperfection of our scientific instruments, which can, however, be made less and less imperfect. Newton did not think that the use of mathematical syntheses *a priori* would give us the absolutely true laws; he felt that the mathematical formulations which he gave to physical laws were not perfect; e. g. he noted that the laws of refraction, because they are geometrical, are susceptible of different mathematical expressions. New experience may always modify the formulae and make them more precise. Newton knew that it would be very difficult, if not impossible, to express all of the diverse causes of nature giving rise to one effect in terms of a single and final mathematical formula. These laws are, however, for Newton, *objective*, even if their expression in terms of a mathematical generalization is imperfect and limited ; *they are objective representations of the relationships that exist in nature, but are limited, because of our imperfect knowledge of facts.* The plurality of causes and relations in nature are many, and our knowledge of them is small ; in fact, Newton said that the laws really deal with relations, which are mathematical, and not with the causes, which need not be mathematical.[1]

Like Galileo, Newton believed rightly that these mathematical formulae must be modified as knowledge progresses, even his universal law of gravity. A mathematical formula is usually a first approximation to the truth. It may then pass through a *series* of further approximations, with the truth as the possibly never-attained limit. Yet that truth is itself no less precise, though more complex than the approximate formula. Therefore, for Newton, natural laws are objective, perfect, and immutable, though our knowledge and expression of them may be imperfect, but we come to know them more perfectly in proportion

[1] Newton, *Mathematical Principles of Natural Philosophy*, English translation by A. Motte, 1st ed., London, 1729, Book II, Sect. vii, Prop. 37, 36, Cor. 4. See also second and third books of Newton's *Optics*.

to our scientific knowledge of the world. As Newton says : ' Most celebrated Philosophers of Greece and Phoenica who made a Vacuum, and Atoms, and the Gravity of Atoms, the first Principles of their Philosophy, tacitly attribute Gravity to some other cause than dense Matter. Later philosophers banish the consideration of such a cause out of natural Philosophy, feigning Hypotheses for explaining all things mechanically, and referring other causes to Metaphysics. Whereas the main Business of Natural Philosophy is to argue from phenomena without feigning Hypotheses and to deduce causes from effects, till we come to the very first cause, which certainly is not mechanical . . . and, though every step made in this Philosophy (Natural Philosophy) brings us not immediately to the Knowledge of the first Cause, yet it brings us nearer to it, and on that account is to be highly valued.' [1]

It is now clear that the foundation of Newton's mathematical physics was free from any hypothesis assuming first or final causes. In fact, he even went so far in his attempt to free his physics from any metaphysical implications as to lay down a dictum *Hypotheses non fingo*. He did that, however, after a bitter polemic against him by the

[1] Newton, *Optics*, 3rd ed., London, 1721, Qu. 28 ; see also Qu. 30, 31.

Cartesians—Hooke, Huygens, Lucas, Cassegrain, Pardies, and others.[1] They all opposed Newton's use of hypothesis, especially the one to be found in the thirty-first question of the *Optics*. But this dictum did not mean for Newton precisely what it literally says. In Newton's physics and optics we can find two types of hypothesis. The first, which is simple, easy to use, and natural, is the hypothesis upon which the atomic theory rests, the theory of undulation and emanation. This type of hypothesis is based as nearly as possible on the totality of observations after the analysis of observed facts of nature has been completed. In a well-developed science this kind of hypothesis becomes fact or disappears. The second is a complex hypothesis, which is made in order to complete a system. This type of hypothesis may be contradicted by the fact which it claims to represent, as in the case of Newton's early theory of light. Newton believed that hypotheses should be used in order to make new discoveries. According to either definition, then, hypothesis is made after certain facts have been analysed ; by the use of this hypothesis a set of deductions are made and verified fully or partially. These hypotheses must be, Newton thought, (1) clearly expressed ; (2) they should follow ex-

---

[1] See above, Chapter III.

perience, and never come before ; (3) they must be suggested by the facts of experience ; (4) they must be formal ; (5) they must not contradict the three rules laid down for all mathematical physics : (*a*) that we must not admit more causes than are true and are needed to explain the facts, (*b*) that we must ascribe equal causes to equal effects, (*c*) and, finally, that the qualities of bodies which cannot be lessened or reinforced, and which are found to be true of bodies that we have actually experienced, are true of all bodies. In the last point Newton unconsciously assumed an important law of induction, a law which is really a speculative hypothesis.

Another assumption (6) which Newton made unconsciously, and which really is a dogmatic hypothesis, is in his use of mathematical concepts of relationship between phenomena—his assumption that the nature of physical facts corresponds step by step with the deductions employed in mathematical correlation of propositions. Even though we should begin our mathematical chain of deductions with general propositions which were the result of our observations of nature, and if also the resultant propositions were verifiable, nevertheless, the intermediate steps employed in our calculations may or may not have any correlations whatsoever with the world of physical phenomena. Newton, however, employing mathematics as a method of procedure, presupposed this general hypothesis that each step in a mathematical demonstration is true of the physical world.

Finally, (7) a good hypothesis for Newton does not attempt to answer the *why* but the *how* of facts, the *form* and not the *essence* of nature. The reason for this position on Newton's part was a traditional belief in a providential non-mechanical order, which for him was the final explanation of the universe. Such an *essence* would never be supplied, Newton thought, by science or natural philosophy in its development at his time, if ever. Newton believed that it may be hoped for when all of scientific knowledge is completed, as the final step, but probably it is the business of revealed theology to answer the why and the *essence* of things. In fact, Newton felt that what knowledge we have of God and His attributes is only indirectly attainable from His activity ; never directly, not even by means of reason. So it does not matter what kind of hypothesis we may develop, providing the different types give rise to the same mathematical equation or law : though the *interpretation* of the equation will vary with the different hypotheses, the mathematical form will always be the same. Therefore, the nature of hypothesis is really similar to the nature of definition.[1]

On the other hand, Newton thought, hypothesis should not be used ; (1) as the means of a polemic, as an instrument of criticism ; (2) to develop dogmatic hypotheses in order to make facts fit them ; it is dangerous to oppose facts, even if the use of a hypothesis is only suggestive.[2] That was why Newton is so cautious in suggesting the use of the hypothesis of ' ethereal medium '. This was also why Newton did not place that hypothesis in the main body of his physics or optics, but rather in the form of a question at the end of the *Optics*. The role of this type of hypothesis is to suggest to us the order in our investigation. In the question form Newton could introduce to the scattered facts a hypothesis which may be very suggestive in all further investigations. There is always a time when analysis of facts is so complete that they suggest a law, an order, but which cannot be verified completely nor even partially—the time, that is, when hypotheses are needed to give a directing concept.

We may conclude with the following quotation from Newton's letter to Cotes in reference to his revision of the *Principia*—a quotation which

[1] *Philosophical Transactions*, 1672 (especially p. 5014).
[2] *Ibid.*, 1672 (especially p. 5014).

illustrates the fact that to Newton hypotheses are not metaphysical in aspect but relate entirely to method : ' for preventing exception against the use of the word " hypothesis ", I desire you to conclude the next paragraph in this manner : " for whatever is not deduced from the phenomena is to be called a hypothesis ; and hypotheses, whether metaphysical or physical, whether of occult qualities or mechanical, have no place in experimental philosophy. In this philosophy, particular propositions are inferred from the phenomena, and afterward rendered general by induction. . . . And to us, it is enough that gravity does really exist, and act according to the laws which we have explained, and abundantly serves to account for all the motions of the celestial bodies and of our sea ".' [1]

[1] *A Collection of Papers which passed between the late learned Mr. Leibniz and Dr. Clarke, in the years 1715 and 1716, relating to the Principles of Natural Philosophy and Religion.* Knapton, London, 1717, p. 155.

BIBLIOGRAPHY

This bibliography is not meant to be exhaustive.

Some of the titles contained in this bibliography will be found in more than one section, but no systematic use of cross references has been attempted.

The asterisk (*) before a title indicates a work of special importance.

NEWTON, SIR ISAAC

Writings

NEWTON, SIR ISAAC. *Philosophiae naturalis principia mathematica.* Lond., 1687, ed. R. Cotes; Cantab., 1713; ed. H. Pemberton, Lond., 1726; ed. T. Le Siur et F. Jacquier, Genevae, 1739–42; ed. Coln, 1760; Glasgow, 1822; ed. Wm. Thomson and H. Blackburn, ib., 1871; *Engl.* by A. Motte, 2 vols., Lond., 1729, 1803; id., N. Y., 1848; by R. Thorp, Lond., 1777, 1802; Bk. i, sect. 1–3 by P. Frost, ib., 1854, 1878, 1883; *Fr.* by Madame la Marquise du Chastellet, 2 vols., Paris, 1759; *Germ.* by J. P. Wolfers, Berl., 1872, pp. 666.

—— *Treatise of Optics*, Lond., 1704, 1718, 3rd ed., corr., 1721; 4th ed., 1730; *Lat.* by Saml. Clarke, Lond., 1706, 1719; Lausoduni, 1719, 1740; Patav., 1749; *Fr.* by M. Coste, Paris, 1722, 1739, 1746; *Germ.* by W. Abendroth, series, trans. from Latin by J. Colson, Lond., 1736, 1737; *Fr.* by G. L. Le Clerc, Paris, 1740.

—— *Opuscula mathematica, philosophica et philologica.* Coll. partim que Latine vertit J. Castillionus, 3 vols., Lausoduni et Genevae, 1744.

HORSLEY, SAMUEL, ed. *Isaaci Newtoni opera quae existant omnia*, 5 vol., Londini, 1779–85.

Bibliography 237

(Horsley in vol. i, *Dedicatio ad Regem*, aims to defend
Newton's metaphysical notion of gravity.)

*BENTLEY, R. *Sermons preached at Boyle's Lectures*, &c., ed.
Rev. A. Dyce, Lond., 1838.

(Newton's four letters to Bentley are published in this
collection.)

RIGAUD, STEPHEN PETER. (Though Rigaud's name does not
appear on the title-page, it was he who made this collection.)
*Correspondence of Scientific Men of the Seventeenth Century,
including letters of Barrow, Flamsteed, Wallis, and Newton,
printed from the original in the collection of the Right Honourable the Earl of Macclesfield*. Two volumes (posthumous,
edited by Rigaud's son, Stephen Jordan Rigaud), Oxford,
1841. Table of contents and index added by De Morgan
(see Mrs. De Morgan's *Memoir*, p. 414) in 1862. Fifty-
nine letters from and to Newton, beginning in 1669,
were published on pp. 281–437 of vol. ii.

(Not of great value).

*EDLESTON, J. *Correspondence of Sir Isaac Newton and Professor
Cotes, including Letters of Other Eminent Men, now first
published from the originals in the Library of Trinity College,
Cambridge ; together with an Appendix containing other
unpublished Letters and Papers by Newton ; with Notes,
Synoptical View of the Philosopher's Life, and a Variety of
Details illustrative of his History*. London and Cambridge,
1850.

(Very important, concerning the publication of the
3rd ed. of Newton's *Principia*.)

*BREWSTER, DAVID. (See section on *Life* ; important letters and
short essays by Newton are to be found here.)

BALL, W. W. R. *Essay on Newton's Principia*, 1893.

(Important letters of Newton were published in this
essay.)

JOURDAIN, E. B. *Newton's Hypotheses of Ether and of Gravitation* ; pp. 79 ff., 234 ff., 418 ff. ; *The Monist*, v. 25, 1915.

(Collection of important questions as published in all
the editions of Newton's *Optics*.)

*A Catalogue of the Portsmouth Collection of Books and Papers,
written by Sir Isaac Newton, the Scientific Portion of which
has been presented by the Earl of Portsmouth to the University
of Cambridge.

(This Catalogue was drawn up by the Syndicate
appointed the 6th November 1872, and the preface
is signed by H. R. Luard, G. G. Stokes, J. C. Adams,
and G. D. Livering, and it was published at Cambridge
in 1888.)

*GRAY, G. J. *A Bibliography of the Works of Sir Isaac Newton,
together with a list of Books illustrating his works.* Second
edition was privately printed in 1888.

Life and Works

*BALL, W. W. ROUSE. *A Short Account of the History of Mathe-
matics*, London, 4th ed., 1908.

(In this work, a whole chapter (pp. 319–52) is devoted
to ' The Life and Works of Newton, in which Newton's
early manuscripts are referred to, but without references, and in this chapter the communications with
Leibniz are discussed, but the controversy is dealt
with when an account of Leibniz's work is given
(pp. 353–65), where Leibniz's manuscripts are hardly
referred to, and he himself is treated with suspicion.)

*BREWSTER, DAVID. *Memoirs of the Life, Writings, and Discoveries
of Sir Isaac Newton*, Edin., 1855 ; 2nd ed., 2 vols., 1860 ;
(compiled) Lond., 1864. Cf. *Westm. Rev.*, lxiv. 557 ;
North Brit. Rev., xxiii, 307 ;' id., *Eclectic Mag.*, xxxvi, 717 ;
Brit. Quart., xxii, 317 ; id., *Living Age*, xlvii, 289, 401 ;
Eclectic Rev., cii, 513 ; *Dubl. Rev.*, xxxix, 273 ; *Dubl. Univ.*,
xlvi, 308 ; *J. des Savants*, 1855, Oct., Nov.

—— *The Life of Sir Isaac Newton*, Lond., 1831 ; N. Y., 1845 ;

rev. ed., Lond., 1875 ; *Germ.* B. M. Goldberg, Lpz., 1833. Cf. *Edin. Rev.*, Oct., 1832 ; *J. des Savants*, 1832, avril, mai.

*De Morgan, Augustus. *Essays on the Life and Work of Newton*, Open Court, 1914.

—— Review of Brewster's *Memoirs of Newton* in the *Essays on the Life and Work of Newton*, Open Court, 1914.

[Desaguliers (John Theophilus).] *A Course of Mechanical and Experimental Philosophy*, London, 1723.
> (A Course of Lectures on Newton.)

*Fontenelle, B. Le B. de. *The Life of Sir Isaac Newton, with an account of his writings, &c.*, London, 1728.

Encyclopedia Britannica. Art. ' Newton ', 11th ed., vol. xix, pp. 583 ff.
> (Especially on Atomism.)

*Rigaud, Stephen Peter. *Historical Essay on the First Publication of Sir Isaac Newton's Principia* ; Oxford, 1838. In this book the pages of the text of the first part and those of the Appendix are numbered separately. In the Appendix are given some of Newton's early manuscripts on fluxions from the collection of Lord Macclesfield.

Interpretation

*Addison, J. *Oration in Defence of the New Philosophy . . . at Oxford*, July 7, 1693.
> (Valuable because it reflects the appreciation of Newton's work by his contemporaries as well as by many subsequent writers.)

Abbott, R. *A Short Introduction to the Principia*, London, 1868.

*Abbé D—. *Réflexions sur la physique moderne, ou la philosophie newtonienne comparée avec de Descartes*, Paris, 1757.

Apelt, E. F. *Die Epochen der Geschichte d. Mensch.*, Jena, 1845.

*Baily, F. *An Account of the Rev. John Flamsteed, the First Astronomer Royal, &c.*, 1835.

BAUMANN, J. J. *Die Lehren von Raum, Zeit und Mathematik in der neueren Philosophie . . . Suarez . . . Newton*, Berlin, 1868–9.

*Biographie Universelle. Art. ' Newton ', v. 31.

*BIRCH, THOMAS. *The History of the Royal Society of London*, vol. iii, London, 1757.

*BLOCH, LÉON. *La Philosophie de Newton*, Alcan, 1908.

       (Best study of Newton in a new light, even though the nominalistic tendency is exaggerated.)

*—— *Reviewed* by Prof. G. Milhaud in *Revue de Métaphysique et de Morale*, v. 16, 1908, pp. 492–506. *Supplément*, Jan., 1908, pp. 36 ff. ; mai 1908, p. 10.

       (Useful as a corrective to Dr. Bloch's views on Newton.)

*BOOLE, GEO. *An Address on the Genius and Discoveries of Sir I. Newton*, Lincoln, 1835.

BROUGHAM and ROUTH. *Analytical View of Sir Isaac Newton's Principia*, 1855.

*Commercium Epistolicum, D. JOHANNIS COLLINS et aliorum de Analysi promota : iussu Societatis Regiae, etc., 1712, 2nd ed., 1722.

DIETERICH, K., *Kant u. Newton*, Tubingen, 1877.

DÜRDIK, J. *Leibniz u. Newton*, Halle, 1869.

FICK, A. ' Über den bedeutendsten, Fortschritt der Natur-wissenschaft seit Newton,' *Germ. Rev.* 1884 (1).

*GLAZEBROOK, R. T. ' Sir Isaac Newton ' in *Dict. of Nat. Biog.*, Lond., 1894, xi, 370–93.

GORDON, GEO. *Remarks upon the Newtonian Philosophy*, Lond., 1719.

HARLEY, L. R. *Philosophical Method of Newton, Education*, xvi, 596.

LANGE, F. A. *Geschichte des Materialismus*, Iserlohn, 1866 ; 3 wohlf., Aug., 1887 ; *Engl.* by E. C. THOMAS, Lond., 1877–9 ; *Fr.* by D. Nolen, Paris, 1877–9.

       (This history is of little value for our subject.)

LANGE, LUDW. *Die geschichtliche Entwickelung des Bewegungsbe-griffs*, Lpz., 1886, pp. 47–72.

Bibliography 241

*LASSWITZ, KURD. *Geschichte der Atomistik von Mittelalter bis Newton*, Hamburg, 1890. Cf. *Rev. Philos.*, xxx, 1890, pp. 533–42.
  (The best history of Atomism.)

MABILLEAU, LÉOP. *Histoire de la Philosophie atomistique*, Paris, 1895. Cf. *L'Année philos.*, 1895, pp. 303–4 ; *Rev. philos.*, xlii, 1896, pp. 315–18.
  (This history is of little value.)

MACKENZIE, A. S. *The Laws of Gravitation ; Memoirs by Newton, Bouguer, and Cavendish, together with abstracts of other important memoirs*; trans. and ed. by A. S. M., N.Y., 1900.

MACLAURIN, COLIN. *Account of Sir Isaac Newton's Philo ophical Discoveries*, publ. from the author's manuscript papers by Patrick Murdoch, London, 3rd ed., 1775.

—— *An Account of Sir Isaac Newton's Philosophical Discoveries*, Lond., 1748 ; 2nd ed., 1750 ; *Fr.* by M. LA VIROTTE, Paris, 1749.

MARTIN, BENJAMIN. *Philosophia Britannica*, London, 1759–87.

NEUMANN, C. *Ueb. d. Principien d. Galilei-Newtonisch. Theorie*, Lpz., 1870.

*PAULIAN, A. H. *Traité de paix entre Descartes et Newton*, Paris, 1703.

PEMBERTON, HENRY. *A View of Newton's Philosophy*, Lond., 1728 ; *Germ.* by S. Maimon, Part I, Berlin, 1793.

*PILLON, FR. 'L'Évolution historique de l'Atomisme,' *L'Année philosophique*, ii, 1891, pp. 67–112.
  (Useful history.)

*—— *Critique de l'Atomisme épicurien*, ib., 1897, pp. 85–167.
  (Very good critique.)

POWELL, B. 'Sir Isaac Newton and his Contemporaries,' *Edin. Rev.*, lxxviii, 1843, pp. 402–37.
  (Relation of Newton to Hook.)

ROSSI, G. 'I principii Newtoniani della filosofia naturale,' *Rev. gén. d. Sci.*, ix, 1897, pp. 379–81.

*ROSENBERGER, FERDINAND. *Isaac Newton und seine physikalischen *Principien. Ein Hauptstück aus der Entwickelungs-geschichte der modernen Physik.* Leipzig, 1893.

> (A very able presentation of the actual material of Newton's natural philosophy.)

*ROHAULT, J. *Tractatus Physicus,* London, 1682.

> (Of interest because it is a school text of Newton's physics. It was introduced into the schools because it did not contradict the existence of God.)

SINRAM, A. *Kritik der Formel der Newtonischen Gravitations-theorie,* Hamb., 1896, p. 44.

*SNELL, K. *Newton u. d. mechanisch. Naturwissensch.,* Dresd. u. Lpz., 1843.

STRUVE, A. *Newton's naturphil. Ansichten, G-Pr.,* Sorau, 1869.

*TOSI, J. L. et VANNUCHI, A. M. *Raccolta d' opuscoli sopra l' opinoni filosofiche di Newton.* Firenze, 1744.

VOSS, ALBERT. *Philosophiae naturalis principia mathematica,* Göttingen, 1875.

> (A thesis.)

*VOLKMANN, P. *Newton's ' Philosophiae naturalis principia ma-thematica ' und ihre Bedeutung für die Gegenwart.*

*VOLTAIRE (FRANÇOIS-MARIE-AROUET). *Éléments de philosophie de Newton,* Paris, 1738 ; *Engl.,* Amst., 1738, by J. Hanna, Lond., 1738.

*—— *Dictionn. phil.,* Art. ' Atome '.

*WHEWELL, W. *History of the Inductive Sciences,* London, 1837.

> (A very good section on Newton.)

*WHITTAKER, E. T. *A History of the Theories of Aether and Electricity from the Age of Descartes to the Close of the Nine-teenth Century,* Dublin and London, 1910.

> (A standard history.)

WHISTON, WM. *Sir Isaac Newton's Mathematic Philosophy more easily demonstrated,* Lond., 1716.

WIGAND, J. W. A. *Der Darwinismus und die Naturforschung Newtons und Cuviers.,* Braunschw., 1874.

WRIGHT, J. M. *A Commentary on Newton's Principia*, Lond., 2 vols., 1828.

ZÖLLNER, J. K. F., *Prinzip. d. elektrodyn. Theorie, &c.*, Leipz., 1876.

> (Because of his mystical sense, Zöllner was guided rightly in his understanding of Newton.) See also Isenkrahe, *Das Räthsel von der Schwerkraft.*

NEWTON, ISAAC. *Edin. Rev.*, ciii, 499; id., *Living Age*, xlix, 641; *Chamber's J.*, xxvi, 168, 179; id., *Eclectic Mag.*, xxxix, 531; *Living Age*, lix, 374; *Amer. Quart.*, v. 327; *Edin. Rev.*, lxxvii, 402–37; *For. Quart.*, xiii; *Christ. Exam.*, xii, 277; *Fraser*, vi, 351; *Monthly Rev.*, cxix, 584; cxxvi, 250; *Museum of For. Lit.*, xx, 23, 129; xxii, 157. Precursors of Newton : *Edin. Rev.*, clii, 1880, pp. 1–36.

FORERUNNERS, CONTEMPORARIES, AND DISCIPLES OF NEWTON

Barrows Isaac

BARROWS, ISAAC. The Mathematical Works of Barrows, Isaac. Ed. for Trinity College by W. Whewell, Cambridge, 1860.

—— *Correspondence of Scientific Men of the Seventeenth Century*, including letters of Barrows, Flamsteed, Wallis, and Newton, printed from the original in the collection of the Rt. Hon. the Earl of Macclesfield, 2 vols., Oxford, 1841.

Bentley, Richard

BENTLEY, R. Sermons preached at Boyle's Lectures, &c. Ed. by Rev. A. Dyce, 3 vols., London, 1838.

Boehme, Jacob

SCHIEBLER, K. W., ed. Collected Works of Boehme, 7 vols., 2nd ed., Lpz., 1861 ff. *Engl.* trans. by W. Law, 4 vols., trans. from the 4 vols. 1st ed., Amst., 1620, London, 1764–81.

GICHTEL, J. G., *ed.* *All the Theosophical Writings of Boehme,* 10 vols., Amst., 1682 ; Hamb., 1715.

*DEUSSEN, P. *Jac. Boehme, Ueb. sein Leb. und seine Philosophie,* Rede, Kiel, 1897.
 (Very good address.)

HAMBURGER, J. *Die Lehre des deutschen Philosophen, J. Boehmes,* 1844.

VON HARLESS. *J. Boehme und die Alchimisten,* 1870 ; 2nd ed., 1882.

*HASTINGS, JAMES. *Encyclopaedia of Rel. and Ethics,* Art. ' Boehme ', vol. ii.

PEIP. *J. Boehme, der deutsche Philosoph,* 1860.

PENNY'S *Studies in Boehme,* London, 1912.
 (Not of scientific value.)

Boyle, Robert

*BOYLE, ROBERT. *The Works of the Honourable Robert Boyle,* six volumes ; a new edition, London, 1772.

MEIER, JOHANN. *R. Boyle's Naturphilosophie, mit besonderer Berücksichtigung seiner Abhängigkeit von Gassendi und seiner Polemik gegen die Scholastik,* München, 1907.

STERN, ALFRED. *Ueber einen bisher unbeachteten Brief Spinozas und die Corresp. zwischen Spinoza und Oldenburg, im Jahre,* 1665 (cf. *Works of Boyle,* Bd. V. London, 1744, p. 339), in den Gött. Nachricht, 1872, No. 26.

Encyclopaedia Britannica. Art. ' Boyle ', 11th ed., vol. iv, pp. 354 ff.

Clarke, Samuel

**A* Collection of Papers which passed between the late learned Mr. Leibniz and Dr. Clarke, in the years 1715 and 1716, relating to the principles of Natural Philosophy and Religion* ; London, Knapton, 1717.

*ROHAULT'S *System of Natural Philosophy, illustrated with Dr. Samuel Clarke's Notes ; taken mostly out of Sir Isaac Newton's Philosophy,* London, Knapton, 1723.

Bibliography 245

Descartes, René

Bibliography   245

Descartes, René

DESCARTES, RENÉ. *Œuvres*, Paris, 1824, &c.

—— *Principia philosophiae*, Amst., 1644, vols. i–v.

*ADAM, CHARLES et PAUL TANNERY, *Œuvres de Descartes, publiées par Charles Adam et Paul Tannery, sous les auspices du Ministère de l'Instruction publique*, Paris, 1904 ; vol. viii (*Principia philosophiae*), vols. i–v (*Correspondence*).

*ADAM, CHARLES. *Principes de la Philosophie*, vol. xii, ch. iv, pp. 354 ff. in *Vie et Œuvres de Descartes*, Paris, 1910.

    (A substantial exposé of Descartes's physics.)

Biographie Universelle. Art. ' Descartes ', vol. xi.

BORDAS, DEMOULIN. *Le Cartésianisme*, Paris, 1874 ; Part I, ch. ii, ch. iv, Sect. ii, Part II.

    (Very general.)

*BOUILLIER, FRANCISQUE. *Philosophie cartésienne*, Paris, 1st ed., 1868 ; vol. i, chapters vi, vii, viii, ix.

    (Although an old work, it still has no equal for a general presentation of the Cartesian movement.)

HOFFMANN, A. ' D. L. v. d. Bildung des Universums b. D. in ihrer geschichtl. Bedeutung,' *A. f. G. d. Ph.*, xvii, 1904, pp. 237–71, 371–412.

    (General Cartesian cosmology.)

*SCHNEIDER, HERMAN. *Stellung Gassendis zu Descartes*, Lpz. Diss., Halle, 1904.

    (An able summary of the controversy between the two philosophers.)

*TANNERY, P. ' Descartes, physicien ' ; *Rev. de Mét. et de Mor.*, juillet 1896.

Huygens Van Zuylichen, Christiaan

*HUYGENS VAN ZUYLICHEN, CHRISTIAAN. *Opera reliqua*, Amstelodami, Apud Janssonio—Walsbergios, 1728, Lugduni Batavorum, Apud Janssonios vander Aa, 1724.

* —— *Œuvres complètes*. Publiées par la Société hollandaise des sciences. La Haye : M. Nijohoff 1888.

*HUYGENS VAN ZUYLICHEN, CHRISTIAAN. *Treatise on Light.* Trans. into English by S. P. Thompson, London, Macmillan Company, 1912.

*HUYGENS, YOUNG AND FRESNEL. *The Wave Theory of Light.* New York, American Book Company, 1900.

Kepler, Johann

*KEPLER, JOHANN. *Opera omnia.* Ed. Ch. Frisch. 8 vol. Frankofurti a. M. : Heyder and Zimmer, 1858–70.

*BALDAUF, GEOR. *Kepler Neue Astronomie im Auszuge und in Übersetzung der wichtigsten abschnitte,* Freiberg Gerlachsche Buchdruckerei, 1905–11.

Leibniz, G. W. F.

*LEIBNIZ, G. W. F. *Gesammelte Werke,* hrsg. von C. I. Gerhardt, &c., Hanover, 1843–63, &c.

*—— *Opera omnia,* ed. L. Dutens, 6 vols., Genevae, 1768, &c.

—— *La Monadologie* (1714), publ. *Fr.* by E. Boutroux, Paris, 1881 ; *Engl.* by R. Latta, Oxf., 1898 ; *Germ.* by R. Zimmermann, Wien, 1847.

COUTURAT, L. *La Logique de Leibnitz,* Paris, 1901.
(Best study of the logic of Leibniz.)

*RUSSELL, BERTRAND. *A Critical Exposition of the Philosophy of Leibniz, with an appendix of leading passages* (chaps. iv, vii, viii, x, xi), Cambridge, 1900.
(Shows Leibniz in a new light. Russell gives also an exhaustive bibliography of the works of Leibniz.)

STEIN, LUDWIG. *Leibniz und Spinoza,* Berlin, 1890, pp. 360 ff.

Galilei, Galileo

*GALILEI, GALILEO. *Le opere di Galileo Galilei.* Prima edizione completa, condotta sugli autentici manoscritti palatini. 15 vols. and supplement. O. Firenze : Società editrice fiorentina 1842–56.

*—— *Le opere di Galileo Galilei.* Edizione nazionale sotto gli

auspicii di Sua Maestà il re d' Italia . . . Firenze, tipografia di G. Bardèra, 1891–1909.

*——— *Dialogues concerning two New Sciences*; trans. from the Italian and Latin into English by H. Crew and A. de Salvio . . . with an introduction by A. Favaro. New York, Macmillan Company, 1914.

Gassendi, Pierre

*GASSENDI, PIERRE. *Opera omnia*, ed. by H. L. Hubert de Montmorency and F. Henri; 6 vols., Ludduni, 1658. Ed. by Nic. Averarius; 6 vols., Florent, 1727.

*SORBIÈRE (in the first collected edition of the works, by Bugerel), *Vie de Gassendi*, 1737, 2nd ed., 1770.

    (Life of Gassendi.)

BARNEAUD, TH. *Étude sur Gassendi* (*Nouv. Annales de Phil. cath.*, 1881).

*BERNIER. *Abrégé de la Philosophie de Gassendi*, 8 vols., 1678; 2nd ed., 7 vols., 1684.

BERR, HENRI. *An iure inter Scepticos Gassendus numeratus fuerit*. Lut. Par., 1898.

*BOUILLIER, FRANCISQUE. *Philosophie cartésienne*, Paris, 1st ed., 1868.

    (On Descartes's objections to Gassendi see vol. i, ch. xi.)

BRETT, G. S. *Philosophy of Gassendi*, London, 1908.

Encyclopaedia Britannica. Art. 'Gassendi', 11th ed., vol. vii, pp. 503 ff.

BUHLE, JOH. GOTTL. *Geschichte der neuer Philosophie seit der Epoche der Wiederherstellung der Wissenschaften*, 6 vols., Göttingen, 1796–1804; vol. i, p. 87; vol. iii.

*DAMIRON, PH. *Mémoires pour servir à l'histoire de philosophie au XVIIe siècle*, Paris, 1846.

——— *Histoire de la philosophie au XVIIe siècle*, Paris, 1846.

*FEUERBACH, LUDW. *Geschichte der neuern Philosophie von Bacon bis Spinoza*, pp. 127-50, Ansbach, 1837.

KIEFL, F. X. 'Gassendis Skepticismus' *im Philosophischen Jahrbuch*, v. i, 1893.

*—— P. *Gassendis Erkenntnistheorie und seine Stellung zum Materialismus*, Fulda, 1893.

*SCHNEIDER, HERMAN. *Die Stellung Gassendis zu Descartes*, Lpz. Diss., Halle, 1904.

TAMISEY DE LAROQUE. 'Documents inédits sur Gassendi,' *Rev. des Quest. hist.*, 1877, vol. xxii, pp. 221 ff.

*MARTIN, A. *Histoire de la vie et des écrits de P. Gassendi*, Paris, 1854.

PENDZIG, PAUL. *Pierre Gassendis Metaphysik und ihr Verhältnis zur scholastischen Philosophie*, Bonn, 1908.
  (Sketchy doctoral dissertation like many of the following.)

PFAFF, RUDOLF FRANZ. *Die Unterschiede zwischen der Naturalphilosophie Descartes und derjenigen Gassendis und der Gegensatz beider philosophen überhaupt*, Leipzig, 1905.

PFEIFFER, ADALBERT. *Die Ethik des Peter Gassendi dargestellt und nach ihrer Abhängigkeit von dem Epikureismus untersucht*, Erlangen, 1908.

*RITTER, AUG. HEINRICH. *Geschichte der Philosophie*, x, 543–71, Hamburg, 1829–31.

SORBIÈRE, SAMUEL. *Dissertatio de vita et moribus P. Gassendi* (in *Œuvres complètes*), Lyons, 1658.

THOMAS, F. *La Philosophie de Gassendi*, 1889, Part I.

Gilbert, William

*GILBERT, WILLIAM. *De Magnete, magneticisque corporibus, et de magno magnete tellure ; physiologia nova, plurimis argumentis et experimentis demonstrata* ; Londini, 1600 ; (Berlin, Mayer, 1892) trans. by P. F. Mottelay, N. Y., 1893.

*—— *De Mundo nostro sublunari philosophia nova ; opus posthumus ab authoris fratre collectum pridem et dispositum nunc ex duobus mss. codicibus, editum ex Museio . . . Guilielmi Boswelli* ; Amstelodanii, 1651.

*MUNK. *Roll of the Royal College of Physicians*, 1878.

Bibliography 249

*Humboldt, Alexander. *Kosmos,* Stuttgart, 1845.
(Vol. ii, pp. 727 ff., dealing with terrestrial electricity.)
Encyclopaedia Britannica. 11 Ed. Art. ' Electricity '.
*Poggendorff, Johann Christian. *Geschichte der Physik.,* Leipzig, Barth., 1879, p. 286.

Hobbes, Thomas

*Molesworth, Sir William, ed. *The English Works of Thomas Hobbes of Malmesbury,* London, Bohn, 11 vols., 1839–49.
(vol. i, Elements of Philosophy.)
*Boyle, Robert. *Examination of Mr. Hobbes' ' Dialogus physicus de natura aeris ',* Lond., 1662.
*—— *Dissertation on a vacuum against Mr. Hobbes,* 1674.
*Gühne, Bernh. *Ueber Hobbes' naturwissenschaftlichen Ansichten und ihrem Zusammenhang mit der Naturphilosophie seiner Zeit,* J. D., Leipzig, 1886.
*Kohler, Max. ' Studien z. der Naturphilos. des Hobbes,' *A. F. G. d. Ph.,* xvi, 1903, pp. 59–96.
*—— ' Die Naturphilosophie von Hobbes in ihrer Abhängigkeit von Bacon,' *A. F. G. d. Ph.,* xv, 1902, pp. 370–99.
*——*Hobbes in s. Verhältnis z. der Mechanischen Naturanschauung,* Diss., Berlin, 1902.

More, Henry

*More, Henry. *Enchiridion Metaphysicum, sive de Rebus Incorporeis,* London, Flesher, 1671.
*—— *The Immortality of the Soul, so far as it is demonstrable from the knowledge of nature and the light of reason,* London, 1713.
*—— *An Antidote against Atheism,* London, 1717.
*Hastings, James. *Encyclopedia of Rel. and Ethics,* Art. ' More ', vol. 8.
*Tulloch, John. *Rational Theology and Christian Philosophy in England in the Seventeenth Century,* vol. ii, 2nd ed., 1874.
(One of the best books in that field.)

*WARD, RICHARD. *The life of the learned and pious Dr. H. More*, London, 1710.

(Extensive quotations from More's letters are made by Ward.)

*ZIMMERMANN, R. *Henry More und die vierte Dimension des Raums*, Vienna, 1881.

(An able exposition of More's Doctrine of Space.)

INDEX

Index

Printed in England at the OXFORD UNIVERSITY PRESS
By John Johnson Printer to the University

HISTORY, PHILOSOPHY AND
SOCIOLOGY OF SCIENCE

Classics, Staples and Precursors

An Arno Press Collection

Aliotta, [Antonio]. **The Idealistic Reaction Against Science.** 1914

Arago, [Dominique François Jean]. **Historical Eloge of James Watt.** 1839

Bavink, Bernhard. **The Natural Sciences.** 1932

Benjamin, Park. **A History of Electricity.** 1898

Bennett, Jesse Lee. **The Diffusion of Science.** 1942

[Bronfenbrenner], Ornstein, Martha. **The Role of Scientific Societies in the Seventeenth Century.** 1928

Bush, Vannevar. **Endless Horizons.** 1946

Campanella, Thomas. **The Defense of Galileo.** 1937

Carmichael, R. D. **The Logic of Discovery.** 1930

Caullery, Maurice. **French Science and its Principal Discoveries Since the Seventeenth Century.** [1934]

Caullery, Maurice. **Universities and Scientific Life in the United States.** 1922

Debates on the Decline of Science. 1975

de Beer, G. R. **Sir Hans Sloane and the British Museum.** 1953

Dissertations on the Progress of Knowledge. [1824]. 2 vols. in one

Euler, [Leonard]. **Letters of Euler.** 1833. 2 vols. in one

Flint, Robert. **Philosophy as Scientia Scientiarum and a History of Classifications of the Sciences.** 1904

Forke, Alfred. **The World-Conception of the Chinese.** 1925

Frank, Philipp. **Modern Science and its Philosophy.** 1949

The Freedom of Science. 1975

George, William H. **The Scientist in Action.** 1936

Goodfield, G. J. **The Growth of Scientific Physiology.** 1960

Graves, Robert Perceval. **Life of Sir William Rowan Hamilton.** 3 vols. 1882

Haldane, J. B. S. **Science and Everyday Life.** 1940

Hall, Daniel, et al. **The Frustration of Science.** 1935

Halley, Edmond. **Correspondence and Papers of Edmond Halley.** 1932

Jones, Bence. **The Royal Institution.** 1871

Kaplan, Norman. **Science and Society.** 1965

Levy, H. **The Universe of Science.** 1933

Marchant, James. **Alfred Russel Wallace.** 1916

McKie, Douglas and Niels H. de V. Heathcote. **The Discovery of Specific and Latent Heats.** 1935

Montagu, M. F. Ashley. **Studies and Essays in the History of Science and Learning.** [1944]

Morgan, John. **A Discourse Upon the Institution of Medical Schools in America.** 1765

Mottelay, Paul Fleury. **Bibliographical History of Electricity and Magnetism Chronologically Arranged.** 1922

Muir, M. M. Pattison. **A History of Chemical Theories and Laws.** 1907

National Council of American-Soviet Friendship. **Science in Soviet Russia: Papers Presented at Congress of American-Soviet Friendship.** 1944

Needham, Joseph. **A History of Embryology.** 1959

Needham, Joseph and Walter Pagel. **Background to Modern Science.** 1940

Osborn, Henry Fairfield. **From the Greeks to Darwin.** 1929

Partington, J[ames] R[iddick]. **Origins and Development of Applied Chemistry.** 1935

Polanyi, M[ichael]. **The Contempt of Freedom.** 1940

Priestley, Joseph. **Disquisitions Relating to Matter and Spirit.** 1777

Ray, John. **The Correspondence of John Ray.** 1848

Richet, Charles. **The Natural History of a Savant.** 1927

Schuster, Arthur. **The Progress of Physics During 33 Years (1875-1908).** 1911

Science, Internationalism and War. 1975

Selye, Hans. **From Dream to Discovery: On Being a Scientist.** 1964

Singer, Charles. **Studies in the History and Method of Science.** 1917/1921. 2 vols. in one

Smith, Edward. **The Life of Sir Joseph Banks.** 1911

Snow, A. J. **Matter and Gravity in Newton's Physical Philosophy.** 1926

Somerville, Mary. **On the Connexion of the Physical Sciences.** 1846

Thomson, J. J. **Recollections and Reflections.** 1936

Thomson, Thomas. **The History of Chemistry.** 1830/31

Underwood, E. Ashworth. **Science, Medicine and History.** 2 vols. 1953

Visher, Stephen Sargent. **Scientists Starred 1903-1943 in American Men of Science.** 1947

Von Humboldt, Alexander. **Views of Nature: Or Contemplations on the Sublime Phenomena of Creation.** 1850

Von Meyer, Ernst. **A History of Chemistry from Earliest Times to the Present Day.** 1891

Walker, Helen M. **Studies in the History of Statistical Method.** 1929

Watson, David Lindsay. **Scientists Are Human.** 1938

Weld, Charles Richard. **A History of the Royal Society.** 1848. 2 vols. in one

Wilson, George. **The Life of the Honorable Henry Cavendish.** 1851